HORRIFIC TRAUMATA:
A PASTORAL RESPONSE
TO THE POST-TRAUMATIC
STRESS DISORDER

N. Duncan Sincla

D1198740

SOME ADVANCE REVIEWS

"A gripping, compassionate account of persons who have suffered severe emotional and psychological traumas. A Vietnam vet who has lived through his own hell, Sinclair understands Post-Traumatic Stress Disorder, PTSD. He is primarily interested in comprehending the spiritual needs of the emotionally and psychologically wounded and offering practical suggestions to family and friends seeking to live with and help them. This book will enlighten and sober all persons in the helping professions. It might also provide a balm for survivors who have not been compassionately understood."

Carroll Saussy, PhD
Howard Chandler Robbins Professor
of Pastoral Theology
Wesley Theological Seminary

"Makes a significant contribution to the developing material on Post-Traumatic Stress Disorder. Pastoral ministers will find particularly helpful the stories of individuals which make the pain of this disorder come alive and help one to understand how this disorder is manifested. . . . Contains information to help one respond in a caring and helpful way."

Sister Beth Butler, MSW
Director, Parish Social Ministry
Catholic Social Services, Mobile, Alabama

"Sinclair . . . looked beneath the surface and found a troubled congregation not yet detached from their 'horrible past.' I would encourage every pastor to read this text as a way of getting in touch with the many personal stories which our people bring to us."

Rev. Robert D. Crick
Dean of Ministries
Church of God School of Theology

NOTES FOR PROFESSIONAL LIBRARIANS AND LIBRARY USERS

This is an original book title published by The Haworth Pastoral Press, an imprint of The Haworth Press, Inc. Unless otherwise noted in specific chapters with attribution, materials in this book have not been previously published elsewhere in any format or language.

CONSERVATION AND PRESERVATION NOTES

The paper used in this publication meets the minimum requirements of American National Standard for Information Sciences — Permanence of Paper for Printed Material, ANSI Z39.48-1984.

Horrific Traumata
A Pastoral Response to the Post-Traumatic Stress Disorder

THE HAWORTH PASTORAL PRESS
William M. Clements, PhD
Senior Editor

New, Recent, and Forthcoming Titles:

Growing Up: Pastoral Nurture for the Later Years by Thomas B. Robb

Religion and the Family: When God Helps by Laurel Arthur Burton

Victims of Dementia: Services, Support, and Care by Wm. Michael Clemmer

Horrific Traumata: A Pastoral Response to the Post-Traumatic Stress Disorder by N. Duncan Sinclair

Aging and God: Spiritual Pathways to Mental Health in Midlife and Later Years by Harold G. Koenig

Horrific Traumata
A Pastoral Response to the Post-Traumatic Stress Disorder

N. Duncan Sinclair, MDiv

The Haworth Pastoral Press
An Imprint of the Haworth Press, Inc.
New York • London • (Norwood) Australia

Published by

The Haworth Pastoral Press, an imprint of The Haworth Press, Inc., 10 Alice Street, Binghamton, NY 13904-1580

The quote from Aleksandr Solzhenitsyn is from his book *The Gulag Archipelago* (New York: Harper & Row, 1973), p. 168. Permission received.

Scriptural quotations identified "GNB" are from The Good News Bible with Deuterocanonicals/ Apocrypga, in Today's English Version. © American Bible Society 1966, 1971, 1976, 1979. Used with permission.

Library of Congress Cataloging-in-Publication Data

Sinclair, N. Duncan.
  Horrific traumata : a pastoral response to the post-traumatic stress disorder / N. Duncan Sinclair.
      p.   cm.
  Includes bibliographical references and index.
  ISBN 1-56024-294-9 (acid-free paper).
  1. Post-traumatic stress disorder–Patients–Pastoral counseling of I. Title.
RC552.P67S46   1993
616.85'21–dc20   92-4194
                                                                             CIP

This book is dedicated
to my wife Jean,
who has lived her own life
with me
as we shared love and support
well beyond measure,
even in the midst of much
pain and trauma.

ABOUT THE AUTHOR

N. Duncan Sinclair, MDiv, MA, is an Episcopal priest of the Diocese of Atlanta, Georgia, and a licensed Marriage and Family Therapist. He has worked at the Pastoral Institute and Bradley Center Hospital in Columbus for the past twelve years, and for the past eight years, has specialized in working with trauma victims. Previously, Father Sinclair was a military chaplain on active duty in Vietnam. He is a clinical member of the American Association of Family Therapists and a member of the American Group Psychotherapy Association.

CONTENTS

Foreword

Duncan Sinclair is an excellent pastoral counselor who has specialized in helping traumatized individuals. He does it well. I know this firsthand as a colleague and consultant for his more difficult cases. Now I have discovered he is also a fine writer. He has woven a wonderful book out of personal and professional experiences and it makes for fine reading for anyone, particularly the pastoral counselor and parish minister.

This book is about helping survivors who suffer from the after-effects of horrific trauma. They have suffered through the worst extremes of the syndrome known as Post-Traumatic Stress Disorder (PTSD). Chapter 1 begins with vivid histories about several of Duncan's counselees while he was on the staff of the Bradley Center and Pastoral Institute in Columbus, Georgia. The chapter also introduces the author in a very personal way, as he describes his own trauma in Vietnam. Imagine a young man caught unaware by the Tet Offensive of 1968. The consequences? Indelible memories of death, mutilation, and intense sufferings that changed him forever.

Duncan describes the symptoms of post-traumatic consequences in Chapters 2 and 3. The first symptom is disassociation of horrific past memories and parts of the self from consciousness. Second, the intrusive memories and reenactments of victimization behavior, including self-mutilation. Third, repetitive and timeless post-traumatic symptoms, including flashbacks–the closest thing to insanity there is. Fourth, amnesia and suppression (in order to "keep the lid on" painful memories).

The author then discloses "flashbacks" of his own after he had managed to keep the "lid on" for so many years. That's when he felt overwhelmed by memories which flooded his mind: entering the Army because of unconscious pressures from growing up in a family with four older brothers who had served in the military; the violent confrontation between war supporters and war protesters at Kent State University; and feeling ashamed to wear his uniform the following day at National Airport.

In Chapters 4 and 5, Duncan describes two of the most severe aspects of PTSD: "death of the spirit" and "fragmentation of the self." Those many losses of the self that contribute to the spiritual dysfunction the "death of spirit" include:

- Loss of hope
- Loss of intimacy
- Loss of future
- Loss of peacefulness
- Loss of healing memory
- Loss of spontaneity
- Loss of wholeness
- Loss of innocence
- Loss of trust
- Loss of awe

The most horrific of all post-traumatic consequences is Multiple Personality Disorder (MPD). The average pastor will never know he has seen such a case unless he is receptive and willing to ask his counselee the right questions: Do you have lapses of memory? Do your moods change radically? Do friends or family members ever say that there are times when you seem like there is another person inside of you? Do you ever find yourself someplace and not know how you got there? And then there may just be times when you have an intuitive sense about it: Imagine having a troubled member of the congregation coming into your study one day and all of a sudden the deep feeling begins to surface that you are seeing this person for the first time.

Inexperienced counselors are likely to overlook these warning signs. Such victims have been betrayed and feel a deep sense of shame and distrust of everyone, including helpers, ministers, and God. For this type of situation, readers will be guided by Duncan Sinclair's experiences as a co-therapist in a therapy group that included among others three participants having MPDs. He has found that these patients require lengthy and arduous periods of therapy, which include several phases:

- Becoming known
- Telling and being heard
- Sharing secrets

- Validating the self
- Sharing of rage
- Hope of restoration
- Going beyond the group

In Chapter 6, Duncan examines the repercussions of PTSD. Trauma does not only affect individuals but also families, communities, and nations. History reveals both the impact of trauma on the broader scope of society as well as the transgenerational consequences passed on to children and grandchildren.

Again, Duncan commendably reveals sensitive family issues by describing his son Mark's dream of the coffin, which reflects his fear about the consequences of his brother going to war. In this chapter, Duncan also reveals the nine characteristics of a healthy family:

1. Adaptive ability
2. Commitment to family
3. Communication
4. Encouragement of individuals in the family
5. Expressions of appreciation
6. Religious/spiritual orientation
7. Social connectedness
8. Clear roles
9. Sharing time together

In Chapter 6, Duncan also refers to Charles Figley's five key phases in treating PTSD in families:

1. Building Commitment to the Therapeutic Objectives
2. Framing the Problem
3. Reframing the Problem
4. Developing a Healing Theory
5. Closure and Preparedness

Chapters 7 and 8 address the question How can pastors and counselors help trauma victims? The first step, according to Duncan, is waiting upon the spirit of God, who operates in moments of extremity and perplexity to bring light. He writes: "Perhaps the events of this century have created a condition not unlike PTSD within the psyche of humanity." As a result, Duncan believes there is a trashing of humanity affecting the poor and homeless, the mentally ill, the aborted, and the elderly. He says "PTSD is a growing phenomenon in our time. It is our common illness."

Drawing on his personal experiences again, Duncan describes the special feeling of being linked not only to the survivors of Vietnam, but also to those who reached out to help hundreds and thousands of victims: "I will never lose sight of that sacramental mission in the pouring rain. Buddhist monks, an Episcopal priest, and Army gunships joined together to bring bread to the hungry."

Duncan believes the linking of the world during these traumatic times is enhanced by television: "An industrial gas leak that kills thousands in India. Hurricane Andrew in Florida and Louisiana. A devastating earthquake in Iran. All of these events were televised worldwide just minutes after they happened, providing a common bond of humanity. The revolution that took place in Eastern Europe between 1988 and 1990 and the failed coup in the Soviet Union in the summer of 1991 bound the rest of the world by the intimacy that television can provide."

The second step in helping trauma victims involves pastors' and counselors' and the victims' own reality of God. It is humbling to read Psalm 139:1-16 and become aware of the profound depth of God's knowledge of each of us. It is also important to reread those scriptural references that remind us of how God has entered humanity, particularly how God–The Word–became flesh and lived among us (John 1:14), sharing our pain and teaching us to share in His resurrection.

Third, recovery is linked to channeling God's power through prayer. In Luke 9:29, Jesus drives demons out of a man who was possessed–a man who may have had severe PTSD. Jesus reminded his disciples that they could do the same work, but only with much prayer and fasting. What is prayer? For Duncan, prayer is many things. Sometimes it is simply stating the obvious. Prayer need not be verbal. Prayer certainly includes action. Prayer has radical power to change lives. Prayer transcends time. Prayer links us with God and others, and prayer links us with Jesus' pain on the cross as well as with His heavenly banquet feast.

Fourth, Duncan states that recovery is facilitated by the healing power of relationships. However, counselors must also recognize that there will be times when "no one of us can possibly relate in therapeutic ways with all people."

Fifth, recovery is also facilitated by a skilled and humble counselor or therapist. Duncan makes it clear that there are two cardinal rules for those who help victims and survivors: (1) Know your own limitations, and (2) Share with another professional your honest feelings related to your counseling and the counselee. He writes: "Applying these two cardinal rules will help to reduce, by a significant level, the amount of harm that may be done in a helping relationship."

Sixth, recovery is different for different people. The author reminds us that there are two kinds of healings: (1) A return to the same state of health in which the patient was before the disease, and (2) a change that makes the organism better capable of coping with whatever new situation has developed.

Seventh, we can learn a great deal from the Bible. There is much taught about trauma in both the Old and New Testaments. "The killing of Abel by Cain, and the agony of their parents," Duncan writes, is a trauma in which we might begin to see the formation of PTSD symptoms in the heart of the human family." The Old Testament–with its stories of exiles, captivities, and exodus–frequently conveys the loss of hope, trust, and relationships. But the Bible also teaches much about regaining hope. As Duncan writes: "Death and resurrection are at the very essence of the Biblical story in which the reality of lost hope and the promise of hope regained are affirmed over and over again."

Helping those who are recovering trauma victims is a challenging and worthwhile effort. Recovery does not happen overnight. In fact, for many victims and survivors, recovering from trauma is an involved journey that requires patience and commitment. I am one who believes that the journey should include a spiritual approach to life, with reliance on God's help and direction. Reading this book will help you accomplish this. It is a book that no pastoral counselor should be without.

Joel Osler Brende, MD
Co-author, *Vietnam Veterans: The Road to Recovery*

Preface

The genesis of this book is from the heart of a sensitive, caring, and wounded healer. The author has gifted us with a rare and intimate look into his own horrific experiences as well as those to whom he has ministered. This book exposes the stark and terrible reality of trauma, with no hint of superficiality or sensationalism. One can feel the agony of the author as the issues of evil, pain, and death are squarely faced. There are no easy answers here. The author has too much honesty and integrity for reiterating superficial pious clichés. However, he does offer hope–a hope that is generated in the hearts, minds, and wills of fellow strugglers courageously facing together their varied traumatizing experiences. Through these shared experiences, the hope and healing are born and nurtured. Those who have experienced trauma and those who seek to minister to trauma victims will find *Horrific Traumata: A Pastoral Response to the Post-Traumatic Stress Disorder* disturbing at times, but clearly helpful and always hopeful.

Wayne Hill, PhD
College of Human Sciences
Florida State University
Tallahassee, Florida

We Are Each of Us, Cells or Particles in the Corpus
Mysticum of a Divine Universe.

-G. Adler

If only it were all so simple!
If only there were evil people somewhere
insidiously commiting evil deeds
and it were necessary only to separate them
from the rest of us and destroy them.
But the dividing line between good and evil
cuts through the heart of every human being,
and who is willing
to destroy a piece of his own heart?

-Aleksandr I. Solzhenitsyn, *The Gulag Archipelago*

I do not ask how the wounded one feels, I myself become
the wounded one.

-Walt Whitman, *Leaves of Grass*

Introduction

The violence of the Vietnam war enabled us to regard victims of severe emotional and psychological trauma with a new understanding and a better ability to heal the awful effects of the trauma. Joining the ranks of traumatized veterans are victims and survivors of incest, rape, hostage situations, and violence of unspeakable kinds. These, and a myriad of others, are now designated as persons who experience Post-Traumatic Stress Disorder (PTSD).

Every parish setting has a group of folks who no doubt stand on the edges of the parish or who have been left to live in their own darkness–victims too filled with pain, shame, anger, and rejection to rejoin the mainstream of ordinary living.

The effects–the fallout–of the victimization are too often so removed in time from the events of the victimization itself that cause and effect are no longer seen. As a result, the victim suffers unknowingly, all too often unaware that her victimization is not of her own creation. Life stressors open past wounds in ways that leave the victim vulnerable to severe pain, without awareness of its cause. The victim then fills in this void of unknowing with shame, hopelessness, and guilt.

Our culture rewards "pulling yourself up by your own bootstraps" or "turning it over to Jesus." For the victimized, neither of these two approaches is helpful. To nurture victims to heal and to relieve the pain of gross victimization requires a greater commitment to understanding and healing than either of these two cultural slogans implies. Because the parish is the center of forgiveness and grace, it must be ready to receive victims into the arms of the "Saving Victim," namely, Jesus the Christ.

For many reasons, our age is increasing in the severity of its violence. Safe havens are fewer and fewer. The rural pastoral setting of years past, with unlocked doors and neighbors who cared, ended with Norman Rockwell. Chained and bolted doors and latchkey kids have become the norm. Violent domestic crime has increased with awful results. Victimization of persons, from preschool children suffering incest to "granny-bashing," is now part of our everyday lives. Gang rapes and beatings are commonplace, and many are done "just for the fun of it." The taking of hostages for political or personal gain is increasing. Mass murders and random shootings heighten our need to be more competent in our ability to deal with the awful results of victimization.

Clergy of all levels–parish clergy, chaplains, pastoral counselors, and indeed all people who provide care–need to develop heightened awareness of the life pain that victims of violence suffer. In addition to a growing awareness, a well-practiced response to the pain of victims needs to be maintained. The literature in this field is growing daily. Whatever the trauma, the pathology is the same, the treatment is the same, the need for compassion and healing is the same, and the mistreatment in the aftermath of victimization is too often the same.

The religious community is a natural haven for the victims of severe trauma. Too often, however, the community's response may not only be inadequate, it may also create even greater harm. We need to be reminded again and again that the Church is a sanctuary for human brokenness. Persons with AIDS stand in our midst as a powerful reminder of the very mixed record of the Church's relationship with the community of human brokenness. Human nature all too often demands that the victim be blamed. The young child who is a victim of incest believes she is "bad" and so will not tell anyone what happened. The rape victim hides her violation and pain because she feels overwhelming shame. The Vietnam veteran does not talk, and perhaps even lies, about his service in Vietnam. Psychiatrist Bessel van der Kolk describes the often debilitating effects of victimization:

> The essence of psychological trauma is the loss of faith that there is order and continuity in life. Trauma occurs when one loses the sense of having a safe place to retreat within or outside oneself to deal with frightening emotions or experiences. This results in a state of helplessness, a feeling that one's actions have no bearing on the outcome of one's life. Since human life seems to be incompatible with a sense of meaninglessness and lack of control, people will attempt to avoid this experience at just about any price, from abject dependency to psychosis. Much of human

endeavor, in religion, art, and science, is centrally concerned with exactly these grand questions of meaning and control over one's destiny.[1]

To be the victim of severe emotional trauma is to have a severe crisis of faith ("My God, My God, why hast thou forsaken me"). There is no restoration of faith or rebuilding of hope apart from a community of faith and hope.

This book is written to share stories of persons whose meaning, faith, and hope were ripped from them by others. The stories are all true stories of men and women of courage. The stories were told to me in an amazing variety of ways. Some were told with a flood of tears and words in a matter of minutes. Some unfolded following years of preparation. Others were acted out without words. Some were only hinted at. Each was told with that particular grace that comes only from suffering, a suffering that is very recognizable once you have looked into the eyes of broken humanity.

As a chaplain in Vietnam in 1967-68 and 1970-71, I walked for two years in the midst of the unfolding process of gross victimization. Since that period of time, I have lived with my own loss of meaning and faith and have been in the rebuilding process by being in almost daily contact with others of a similar spirit. My instructors have been my own experience and the experience of others. My initial experience in Vietnam was compounded when I returned home to the brokenness of the religious community and to the rejection expressed by many in that community. Mine was not an isolated experience.

Out of all this pain, loss, brokenness, rejection, rebuilding, and healing comes this book, addressed to all of those who have been there and to all who are committed to making the pathway of recovery more available and more healing. The state of the art in ministering to persons who have experienced severe psychological trauma continues to mature and develop. Underlying it always, however, will be the key concepts of compassionate listening, creation of safe places for victims, and restoration of faith and hope. It is my hope and intent that this book will provide some guideposts along the journey from victimization toward wholeness.

The journey that occurred during the writing of this book has been peopled by many friends and loved ones. I have dedicated this book to my wife, and I wish to thank her and our five children and their families for their constant love, care, and concern.

I wish to thank Robert E. Clayton, DO, who gave names to many of the "demons" I shared with him. Personally and professionally, he has offered relief, comfort, and compassion to so very many. Through his faith in me very early on, and against many odds, he welcomed me to walk with him.

I would also like to thank Elie Zeitouni, MD, who offered not only his professional assistance but gave of himself generously.

Too many fellow workers and professionals have been there for me to thank them all individually. I do wish, however, to thank John McCann and Chris Mirskey for their friendship and caring over these past 12 years. To all the others on the Clayton Team and in the Bradley Center, thank you.

To those at the Pastoral Institute, I would like to thank Richard Robertson, who brought me onboard at the PI when I left the Army. To Douglas Turley, who shared many common ways of looking at the world, I am most thankful. I express my gratitude to Gloria Armstrong for the rich life she shared with me as we co-led a psychotherapy group for four years. Her sharing enabled us both to grow in grace. There are too many others to thank in detail, but I would add a most sincere thank you to Deborah Yates, Carol Paris, and Eileen Kalmbach for their rich friendships.

A special thanks goes to Wayne Hill, PhD, who shared with me a great deal of organizational and personal chaos (which we struggled with at times as though they were true demons). Out of this chaos, and a weekly portion of excellent Chinese food, we learned the value of true and lasting friendship.

I wish to thank William Clements, PhD, my editor, for his trust and acceptance of me as a potential writer.

To Betty Clements, a very special thank you. She met this manuscript just as she moved from Georgia to California, and she has struggled to give life to words that often had none.

Finally, and with humility, I want to thank the men and women who entered my life and not only told me their stories, but also gave me the courage to write this book.

N. Duncan Sinclair

NOTE

1. van der Kolk, Bessel A., Ed. "The Psychological Consequences of Overwhelming Life Experiences," in *Psychological Trauma* (Washington, D.C.: American Psychiatric Press, 1987), pp. 2-3.

Chapter 1

The Nature of Trauma

THE STORY OF KATE

"Mommy, where are you? I'm stuck, Mommy! I can't get out. I'll be good–just don't leave me here! They're biting my feet again!! Let me out!!! I'm sorry I let Daddy do that to me–just let me out!! I won't tell. I promise I'll never, never tell. I'll never tell anybody. Just let me out! I'm very, very afraid!" Oh God, I'm in the coffee shop, she said to herself. What happened? Am I alone? What have I been saying? The time? What day? Where am I supposed to be? Maybe if I call . . .

Kate* left the restaurant and went on to work too stunned and too fearful of her experience to talk about it. It was terribly familiar, like severe nausea that came and went without explanation. It kept coming back with sickening regularity. The lost periods of time, and the fear and panic that followed, had been with her for years.

The next Thursday in group psychotherapy, Kate was able to make some sense out of the experience. The lights in the elevator she was on had gone out and she had been alone in the dark, closed space; that was the last she remembered until she found herself sitting in the coffee shop. This is what the group called a flashback–reliving the past in a present moment, with the full impact of the past reexperienced.

Kate is a young woman who was betrayed by both parents early in life. The second of two children, she had an older brother. Between the ages of 6 and 12, she had repeatedly been sexually molested by her father with full penetration. When evidence of the incest became known, Kate was punished by her mother. She was locked in a dark upstairs closet for hours, sometimes all day. She was forced to own the guilt, to be responsible for her own wrongly assumed guilt and for

---

*All names, identifying characteristics, and other details of the case material in this book have been changed.

her father's real guilt. Kate not only lost the love and care of her father, she lost the nurture and protection of her mother. She was punished for her losses over and over again for about six years. The nights of pain and brutal agony she experienced with her father were intensified many times by the certainty that the next day she would be severely punished by her mother for her father's brutality. Living with tormentors instead of parents, she found no comfort in her older brother, who was forced by his parents to be the "good" child. Her pain was not eased when she prayed in church, along with her parents, "Our Father, who art in heaven. . . ." She found no comfort either in the presence of the Virgin, "the Mother of God."

Kate left home following high school and found freedom for a time. Sharp divisions between good and evil had been created in Kate's life. The nights of pain and horror and the days of airless abandonment could never be connected with the normal, happy life of her family as it appeared to outside observers. After she left home, the evil eventually became almost unreal, fading into the shadows of memory that had difficulty recreating the horror she had known. The long, brutal nights and the dark, vermin-filled days in the closet became like scenes from a long-ago horror movie. Little or no feeling was left in her, and these scenes from the past became more unreal, even unbelievable. The horror became so suppressed and "resolved" that when Kate was asked about trauma in her life, she would reply with a smile and say with sincerity, "I had a happy childhood. We were a normal family."

THE STORY OF TONY

Tony got up from the supper table and walked to the front yard. It had been a hard day, but he felt very good now and looked forward to watching a football game on TV in a half hour. He said to his mother-in-law, "You know what, Mom? That daughter of yours has learned to cook cornbread just like you. After a meal like that, I'm ready to kick back and watch the game. Today I was handling 30,000 volts at work with a bunch of new guys, and it sure wrecked my nerves." He noticed his son playing in the street. "Hey, little guy," Tony called to him, "bounce that ball on the sidewalk, not in the street!" Tony turned back to his mother-in-law. "Is Dad in the garden?" he asked her. "I think I'll walk down and visit with him before the game."

"Betty! Betty!" The voice came from around the side of the house. It was Tony's father-in-law calling for his wife. He apparently wanted to show her something from the garden.

What the hell! The sun's coming up! What happened to the night? My legs won't move! My arms–they're covered with bites. That stench, where did it come from? Why am I holding this stick? My hands won't bend. They won't move! Last night? Supper? The kid in the street? Mom? Where? Why? Why? Why? Why won't it end? Why night after damn night? He forced himself to stand, and then walk the mile back to the house from the tree line at the edge of the cotton field.

Tony went in, ate breakfast, got ready for work, and left without saying a word. It was too painful and it happened too often to talk about. Last night was a repeat of many nights over the last five years. They had begun shortly after the birth of his son a few years after Tony returned from Vietnam.

Several nights later, in his Vietnam Support Group, Tony pieced it together. His son's bouncing ball and his father-in-law's calling, "Betty! Betty!" added up in his mind to that awful wartime alarm, "Bouncing Betty!!!!" The Bouncing Betty was that terrifying landmine that came up out of the dirt and cut human bodies in half and maimed those farther back, taking off arms and legs. Once he "heard the alarm," he spent another night of Vietnam warfare in a Georgia cotton field.

Tony had left home at the age of 18 to join the Army, to try to create a future out of a childhood that had been blunted by poverty and domestic violence. No one cared when he left–daily survival was consuming too much of everyone's energy for them to notice. The companionship and the team spirit of the Army filled an emptiness in his life. For the first time ever, he felt that he belonged, and found meaning in his life. Following basic and advanced infantry training, Tony was sent to Vietnam and joined the 101st Airborne Division. A young man without family and without meaning, Tony found both in the context of the Army. Tony believed the 101st Airborne Division was "the place to be." He was on his first patrol in the field, afraid but feeling well prepared, when the unthinkable happened. His squad came upon a young American soldier staked to the ground and skinned alive. He had been left there by the North Vietnamese to be found by his fellow American soldiers. Tony never forgot the horror and the terrible questioning in the wide-open, death-filled eyes. Life would never be the same for Tony.

Until Tony's recent death in a motorcycle accident, that awful moment in Vietnam 20 years ago shaped and molded his life. The war, fought over and over again in the hot and humid Georgia nights, had never ended for Tony. The violence, rage, hatred, and brutality that followed that first day in the jungle were replayed again between the happy moments of returning home, getting married, and raising two children. Prior to his death, Tony found a measure of relief, in his work at a Veterans' Administration Hospital and in his participation in the local Vietnam Veterans Support and Therapy Group. The relief came in sharing the torment he had known for the past 20 years with others who had some degree of understanding. Their understanding came from the ghosts in their own lives that had been created by their own wartime traumas. Each member of the group, on learning of Tony's death, asked the same question in his own heart, "Did Tony choose to die in order to stop the pain?"

POST-TRAUMATIC STRESS DISORDER

Kate and Tony did not know each other, but they shared the full impact of a condition known as Post-Traumatic Stress Disorder (PTSD). Kate and Tony are representative of the many people who are active in any local parish. Their stories are usually not known to the pastor, since the stories are too confusing and too frightening to tell. More often than not, these stories remain private until they burst out into the open with surprising consequences. Over and over again, the victim is revisited by the crushing reality of their past trauma, which leaves them helpless as they relive–not just remember–a slice of their own personal story. It may be relived in seconds, as when Kate rode down in the elevator, or extended and relived throughout the night, as in Tony's case. In either instance, the experience is profoundly real on all levels of the person's being.

Trauma is the common theme in Kate's and Tony's lives. Trauma is the cause, the creator, of the emotional condition of their lives.

Trauma wipes away a lifelong accumulation of security and trust and leaves one irrevocably changed.

There is much that is traumatic about life. We all carry our own level of it to varying degrees. This book, however, deals with the profound trauma that is outside the boundaries of ordinary living. Such trauma is usually not confronted in the course of daily life. The trauma that Kate and Tony knew is produced by a horrific event, or series of events, that rips away innocence, trust, security, and caring and leaves gaping holes of disbelief, horror, and fear. It is, of course, known by ordinary people, but always in other than normal circumstances. It is known by ordinary people who find themselves in the wake of events that are outside the bounds of daily living (such as incest or war).

THE HISTORY OF POST-TRAUMATIC STRESS DISORDER

It is surely ironic that wars bring not only killing and wounding but new ways of treating the wounds. The Civil War brought morphine into use. Addiction to morphine became known as the "Soldier's Disease." Since that time, morphine has made a major contribution to the medical management of pain. World War II brought with it many advances in modern medicine, including the development and use of sulfa drugs and the advent of antibiotic medicines. The Korean War brought with it the development of the MASH unit, a mobile surgical hospital that has excellent use in so many types of civilian emergency situations. The Vietnam War brought an understanding of the concept of PTSD and some initial ways of treating it. In the treatment of Vietnam veterans, it was not long before it became clear that the concept, process, and treatment of PTSD applied to an overwhelming number of civilian conditions as well. But this is getting ahead of the story. We need to go back a few years to the war itself and to some of the events that followed it.

Toward the end of the Vietnam War, military psychiatrists published reports stating that the Vietnam War was a major exception to other wars the United States had been involved in. This was so, they said, because of the greatly reduced number of psychiatric casualties. The teams of military mental health providers (and their significant use of minor tranquilizers) were credited with this reduction in psychiatric casualties. Emotionally disturbed soldiers were not shipped out of the country, they were returned to their units as soon as possible. Rest and Recuperation, the famous R&R, and the fixed length of the tour in Vietnam were designed to reduce the number of emotional and mental casualties. Toward the end of the war, and for a short period after it ended, it looked as though this system had worked. What was not known then was the fact that psychiatry did not have a category to understand the peculiar nature of the severe emotional and mental condition that the Vietnam War had generated. It was only some years after the war that veterans themselves began to identify their own disordered lives, and this process began to be incorporated into the works of Chaim Shatan, Robert Jay Lifton,[1] and others who did original and creative work in the field.

Chaim Shatan, in his seminal work in this field, reminds us that "grinding horror" as a daily reality will eventually pervade the whole reality of a person's being.[2] The horror is no longer "out there"; it has invaded the fabric of the person's own life and is now a part of his reality. With this eventually comes a "radical personality change," brought about by the reality of ongoing threats of death and/or torture. Mutilations, killing, and threats of being killed all contribute to the eventual radical change of personality.

Dr. Shatan reminds us that a soldier's coming home does not end the struggle. Ex-soldiers come home to die, to commit suicide, to sit and stare "the thousand-mile stare" for years to come. Eventually, the most common response is a "new constricted adaptation to life," an adaptation based on the "intertwining of savagery with desperate anxiety" that remains unresolved. He calls it the "survivor's tattered garment," which is "unhealed psychic reality–a reality that has never been fully restructured. This is his specific wound." The soldier's identity remains connected with the reality of the destructive world from which he has come. There, Shatan writes, "psychotic reality was the norm, eclipsing the reality of everyday living." With little separating the two realities, the traumatized soldier easily "adopts the paranoid posture and mentality necessary for survival." For years to come, the past malevolence can overwhelm the present reality. What enabled the soldier to survive during wartime is neither paranoid nor strange to him, only to outsiders. Shatan writes: "People's haunting experiences are stitched into the tapestry of their lives." When a soldier returns home or to safety, he must make the transition from facing possible death to facing everyday reality. To do so requires that huge chunks of reality be dissociated from experience. The result is a "perceptual dissonance." Out of this dissonance come the many symptoms of the disorder that are in essence "impulses which have had to be restrained, yet press constantly for utterance."

When the American Psychiatric Association published the third edition of its *Diagnostic and Statistical Manual of Mental Disorders*[3] (commonly known as DSM III) in 1980, the book contained a new diagnostic category called "Post-Traumatic Stress Disorder." In part, this new category described the type of emotional problems that came out of the Vietnam War and that were then being recognized and treated to some degree. This diagnostic category was, however, certainly not confined to Vietnam veterans. It addressed a whole range of conditions affecting people who had survived in the face of extraordinary circumstances.

In 1985, the first annual meeting of the Society of Traumatic Stress Studies was held in Atlanta, Georgia. In addition to the wide range of professionals in attendance, there were also many trauma survivors and helpers (and some of whom were both). All participants came together to foster a professional society committed to the study and treatment of people who were survivors of inhuman conditions in a human world. At the meeting, there were people who had given years of personal and professional counseling to victims of incest. There were women who had given their personal and professional time to victims of rape; these women also shared their concerns, research, and skills with those attending. There were men and women who had committed years of work to the survivors of natural disasters. People who had given years of work in the field of domestic violence came and stood alongside those already mentioned. People who worked with hostages and other victims of violent crime also came to learn and to contribute their learning.

POST-TRAUMATIC STRESS DISORDER TODAY

Out of the first Society of Traumatic Stress conference came a strengthening of the community of professionals and lay people who are committed to the understanding and care of trauma victims. (The

Society now publishes the *Journal of Traumatic Stress.)* At its fall meeting in 1990, the Society changed its name to reflect a wider range of work, and it is now known as the International Society for Traumatic Stress Studies. As part of this work, a group of society members who served in the Vietnam War traveled to the Soviet Union, where the group worked and shared its experiences with Afghanistan War veterans and with the Soviet government. Commonality and community have been discovered and nurtured through similar work. Yael Danieli and the Center for Holocaust Studies in New York have contributed years of experience and research to this developing field.

TYPES OF TRAUMATA AND THEIR VICTIMS

The surprise results of these shared experiences has been confirmation that horrific traumata inflict upon their victims a common condition. The Jewish grandmother in a New York nursing home who has Nazi death-camp numbers tattooed on her forearm and who now, after years of peace, suffers rage and nightmares is not unlike the young woman who wakes up in a cold, dread-filled sweat because she is terrified by nightmares of her nursing duty in Vietnam. Kate and Tony, mentioned at the beginning of this chapter, have much in common with former members of an airline crew who were held hostage; the ex-crew members now drink nightly in order to sleep, to be ready for the mundane jobs they now hold because the hostage incident forced them to leave their airline careers behind. Often, survivors find it next to impossible to leave the safety of their homes. The Vietnam veteran and the schoolchild whose classroom was shattered by automatic-rifle fire both see strangers in a different light. The child who is a helpless witness to his mother's brutal rape is a child marked for life. The young woman who sees her father beaten and then murdered is radically changed, and she will live with these changes for the rest of her life.

No parish is without its trauma victims who seem to live ordinary lives, having returned, apparently safe, from an inhuman world. When we consider all the types of victims discussed above–along with the countless others who have experienced group trauma in a wide variety of ways–the category of victims grows to serious proportions. Our age still lives with the memories of the atom bomb. The plight of the Haitian Boat People is a sad reminder that political trauma continues unabated. The threats of South American drug lords to shoot schoolchildren unless governments back down from drug reform remind us that the Church will house the broken in spirit for years to come. No discussion of horrific traumata would be complete without an acknowledgement that institutional racism creates generational trauma that is indeed way beyond that of ordinary living. With this in mind, it is not too much to say that any horrific trauma inflicted on a person of minority status or a women will have greatly increased effect due to the inherent trauma of racism or gender prejudice already present before the event and which remains even after the trauma.

In later chapters, we will consider in detail the generational effects of trauma, but we do need to note now that each generation is shaped by the experiences of the past. Hoards of refugees in Europe and Asia have, together with their parents and grandparents, known little but war and the effects of war all of their lives. Incest and domestic violence move along the generational chain until they begin to take on a natural character of their own. Erich Fromm reminds us in his classic *Sane Society* that in time we begin to consider humanity's inhumanity as a natural force and war becomes as inevitable as floods and earthquakes.[4]

We also need to consider the magnitude of traumata created by our industrial "advances." Mine accidents stand as the hallmark of family and community trauma. The night before I wrote this section, yet another mine accident was reported in Kentucky. The tragedies of Chernobyl in the Ukraine and Bhopal in India find meaning as they become symbols of humanity's industrial inhumanity. The near misses of Three Mile Island and other places remind us of the industrial Russian roulette being played in thousands and thousands of places on Planet Earth.

Above all, we need to learn that there is in our midst a community of survivors who suffer:

> Until recently, the consequences of specific traumas–such as wars, concentration camp experiences, rape, civilian disasters, and child abuse–were generally described as separate entities. However, closer examination makes it clear that the human

response to overwhelming and uncontrollable life events is re-markably consistent. Although the nature of the trauma, the age of the victim, predisposing personality, and community re-sponse all have an important effect on ultimate post-traumatic adaptation, the core features of the post-traumatic syndrome are fairly constant across these variables.[5]

THE STORY OF ANN

Ann is a 35-year-old woman who was brought into an alcohol and drug treatment center for treatment of a serious alcohol abuse and dependence condition. She had been drinking heavily for the past five years, with increased tolerance and increased consumption. She was drinking about two six-packs of beer daily; on weekends, she would also consume several pints of vodka. She has been arrested twice for driving while intoxicated. Ann and her husband were divorced three years ago, and her 17-year-old son lives with her mother in an infor-mal arrangement that seems to be acceptable to both Ann and her ex-husband. Ann continues to work as a legal secretary but has been counseled on the job on three different occasions. Ann's case looked like a straightforward one of alcohol treatment. During the third week of treatment, however, when most patients look alive and very posi-tive, Ann seemed to lose the positive spirit we expected to see follow-ing the early withdrawal period. She was angry, accusatory, and wanted to leave treatment. During the fourth week, she shared the following information. Fifteen years ago–five years before her mar-riage and seven years before the birth of her son–Ann had been abducted from a downtown parking lot. She had been taken to a wooded edge of town, where she was raped repeatedly over a six-hour period by two escaped convicts. Eventually, she was able to escape. By the time she met her husband, she had sat through two public trials. Since then, she has done her best to forget, to disengage, to deny the whole experience, but above all to stay numb, saying, "That's the past and I don't want it in my life."

Ann had not talked about the rape for years. A year before entering treatment, while working in a lawyer's office, Ann typed a rape vic-tim's deposition. Since then, she has had nightmares of her own experience. She has been "seeing" the men who had held her hostage. She has been hypervigilant, estranging herself from her remaining social relationships. One night several weeks prior to treatment, she fired a pistol through her bedroom wall, thinking she saw the men at the foot of her bed. With this new information, it was necessary for both her addiction and her history to be considered in her treatment. Neither condition can be neglected, nor can it be permitted to contribute to the other. The totality of who Ann is became clearer.

Not all addicted people are dealing concurrently with PTSD. However, a high percentage of people who have experienced severe trauma in their lives have at some time used drugs and alcohol to manage their symptoms.

PSYCHOLOGICAL TRAUMA AND HISTORICAL EVENTS

Childhood tales have often dealt with the subject of severe trauma: people who aged a lifetime during hours of crisis, their hair going from black to white in a day's time; people getting trapped in a cave, without hope of rescue; and people who never smiled again after a certain tragedy. Every pastor has at least one story to tell of the home, the room, the desk frozen in time by a mother or widow who could not bare to move past the trauma of loss. In times when the social and personal history of people was better known, it was easier to trace the effects of trauma within the life of a parish and a community. Those frozen moments of time could be better understood.

My own later childhood took place during the years following World War II. In my small community, the bodies of soldiers were brought back both during and after the war. The funerals, held with simple and deeply moving ritual, reminded us all in a very small way of the nature of war. There was the march of the wounded, with their lost legs, their lost arms, their obvious wounds of war. Later came the march of those wounded in their souls. They drank too much. They dreamed awful dreams. They moved frequently, and communities tried to protect them from themselves. There were those who had been prisoners of war. They had their own look of fear: seeing only a part of this world, they seemed not to have left the imprisonment of their past.

Shortly after World War II, Filmmaker John Huston produced a simple, straightforward documentary of the war's psychological casualties; however, the film was classified and locked away by the Department of Defense for 30 years. It was finally released in the early 1980s. I watched the film with a group of fellow mental-health professionals, and we were struck by the fact that these casualties were the ones we had known in our childhood. That we as a nation could not confront the reality of what had happened to these soldiers showed that we were not ready to deal with our own emotional fragility as human beings.

The Korean War brought its own set of emotional casualties, evidenced by the prisoners of war who were "brainwashed" into remaining in North Korea or China and by the prisoners of war who simply turned their faces to the wall and died. American moral fiber was questioned, and President Eisenhower moved to develop the Code of Conduct for the Armed Forces, to "strengthen" our moral backbone and to pretend that humanity has no limits in the face of inhumanity.

With the military successes of World War II and the stalemate of the Korean conflict standing in stark contrast, the aftermath of the Vietnam War caused the nation to develop a ten-year amnesia about it. From the time the pictures were taken of that final, flag-carrying helicopter leaving the U.S. Embassy in Saigon until the dedication of the Vietnam War Memorial in Washington, there was a general dead silence about Vietnam. The exceptions to the silence were issues raised with the trial of Lt. William Calley as well as a growing number of references in movies and TV dramas about "crazed 'Nam vets" (the most notable, perhaps, being Sylvester Stallone's Rambo). In this age, we have inherited a series of shocks to our philosophical systems that should have left us breathless with horror. The Romanticism of the nineteenth century–wherein nature was the revelation of Truth and mankind was the bold expression of all that was good in nature–came to a crushing halt in the trenches of World War I. One soldier could, with one machine gun, kill more of the enemy than a battalion of men could in any previous war.

Honest and honorable men leaped out of buildings on Wall Street in 1929 for perhaps many reasons, but it has been noted many times that some of them jumped because the system they believed in and were committed to had betrayed them. The confidence of the postwar era had been shaken. The Great Depression of the 1930s drove home the point with ever-increasing reality that hope in nature and in political and economic systems was growing more fragile. World War II lifted the hopes of many in the Western World that salvation could come through technology: science in the hands of honorable humanity would save us from evil. Hitler's Panzer Divisions and V2 rockets, the Allies' saturation bombing, the atomic bombs, and the gas chambers were harsh indications that science has no inherent morality. There is no salvation there:

> Once upon a time there were gas
> chambers and crematoria; and no one
> lived happily ever after.[6]

L. L. Langer says of his "modern fairy tale," that "one is compelled to acknowledge the new reality . . . and to rewrite the Little Red Riding Hoods of our youth and past, granting to an amorphous wolf the triumphant role that fairy tales may deny but the history of the Holocaust confirms." Charles Figley writes, "That a country considered among the most civilized and cultured in the western world could allow to be committed the greatest evils that humans have inflicted on humans . . . challenged the structure of morality, human dignity, and human rights, as well as the values that define civilization. The Nazi Holocaust massively and mercilessly exposed the potential boundlessness of human evil and ugliness, in a silently acquiescing world."[7]

Fifty years after the beginning of World War II, we stand dazed by the reality that Planet Earth has been radically disfigured by humanity and humanity's science. In an effort to ease some of this radical pain, drug addiction and its criminal aftermath ravages our youth, our pride, and our future resources.

You have probably noticed that in talking of horrific traumata, we very soon move to talking of evil. I do not apologize for this, but simply acknowledge that it happens. It is not unthinking to say that it is a disorder of our time. As a society, and even as a religious community, we have great difficulty taking evil seriously. We want to pretend that the wolf is in fact toothless and Little Red Riding Hood never was in danger. The common generalization is that the religious conservatives and fundamentalists see evil as trivial, dealing with little of real substance, and that the liberals discount it too easily.

THE STORY OF DUNCAN

Let me share with you the part of my own journey that makes it possible for me to move with relative ease from talking about trauma to talking about evil. I am never fully at ease talking about evil, for I have never quite known what was or was not evil. However, having experienced horrific traumata some 20 years ago, perhaps it is my own "perceptual dissonance," to use Shatan's phrase, that causes me to interchange horrific traumata and evil with some degree of ease.

When I was first in Vietnam, I lived for some three months in a rented hotel in downtown Nha Trang, an old coastal city in central Vietnam that had an unreal quality straight out of some demented mind. Every morning, a mad rush of military jeeps gathered up all the battalion officers and ferried us to the battalion a few miles out of town. At the end of the day, we were transported back through the mass of local humanity to the center of the old city. There, down from the beach in a series of old French-style hotels, lived several hundred Army and Air Force officers. On the roof of our hotel, there was a popular Officers' Club where each night we sat, had dinner, drank, and watched the war far off in the distance. We sat in civilian clothes, not wanting to be a part of that war and hoping against hope that it would all end before it came any closer. We belonged to the Corps Signal Unit and so we knew a lot about the status of the war and military activity across Vietnam. The fighting remained distant, but it was still a few degrees more real than stateside because of our in-country location.

Then we moved from downtown Nha Trang to our new location a few miles south of the city in late January. Somehow this seemed more "Army" and so more real; still, the area was remote, more like Fort Dix than a combat zone in Vietnam. We had a party to celebrate the Chinese New Year. We were told to expect a lot of noise from the city that evening since "the locals will be celebrating New Year's with a lot of noise and excitement. Fireworks and gunfire will be a big part of their celebration, so don't get upset." Tet 1968, the Chinese New Year, had arrived.

I arrived at the compound chapel early the next morning without a clue about what had happened the night before. The phone rang. It was the First Field Force Corps Chaplain, whose office was some miles from us still located down in Nha Trang. He told me, "Get out to the hospital. We're surrounded here and can't get through. The hospital chaplain is desperate for help." I ran over to the battalion headquarters to find a madhouse of activity. In rapid detail, I learned that Nha Trang was under enemy control. Their flag flew over the giant Buddha that was visible from almost every corner of the city.

Then we had our first casualty in the battalion. A young combat photographer from New York had been killed by rifle fire while filming the close fighting in Nha Trang. The battalion commander told me he would see to it that I could attend to those in the hospital as soon as it was declared clear; but at the present time, the road between us and the hospital was blocked with heavy street fighting. Within the hour, I arrived at the 8th Field Hospital in the company of a small convoy just as the First Field Force Commander arrived. Since he knew me from church services, he stopped and said, "Hell of a way to run a truce, Father." He then told me there were a significant number of casualties and that he was appreciative of my being there. He said that another general's driver had been wounded and asked if would I look in on him.

Nothing in my training or imagination could have prepared me for the next eight hours. Innocence, goodness, and sanity all ceased claiming their places in my life at that hour. Walking into the hospital morgue with the Roman Catholic hospital chaplain later that morning was like walking from one reality into the depths of a reality I had not previously known or imagined. More than 20 years later, as I write this, I am not sure if I am recalling the reality of that morning or a synthesis of memories of that morning and many mornings and days that followed. I do know that certain scenes remain as vivid today as they were then.

The young Specialist 4 looked up at me from the floor with a note of surprise in his blue eyes. An attendant yelled that he was not able to keep up with the paperwork, and he wandered aimlessly with a clipboard. Bodies in the hands of litter-bearers continued to come in a side door. They were all Americans. The soldier on the floor continued to gaze up at us with amazement in his eyes. His brains now oozed onto the floor from the gaping hole that had once been the right side of his head. Here was the reality of war that we had been missing all those months on the roof of the hotel. The innocent dead. The mutilation of bodies. Our once-protected psyches were now flooded with undreamed-of horror.

We walked from the rear of the hospital into a courtyard. Here stood two two-and-a-half-ton trucks filled with "enemy" dead. We committed them to God as we had those on the floor of the morgue moments before. I am an Episcopal priest, and the Book of Common Prayer had taught me in many ways of the commonality of death. The gaping holes, the rigidity of death, the stare of horror and amazement in death-filled eyes, the stench, and the finality all confirmed what the Prayer Book had poignantly noted:

> Rest eternal grant to them, O Lord;
> And let light perpetual shine upon them.
> May their souls, and the souls of all the departed,
> through the mercy of God, rest in peace. Amen.

This prayer needed to be said often because there was no peace during these days filled with death.

The rest of the day was committed to watching others die. They died too fast to be moved out quickly. The frantic staff relied on its training to help handle the crisis as efficiently as possible. It would be nights and nights and years and years later before this scene, compacted by countless others that were to follow, came oozing out of my unconscious.

The first night back with my unit, an older warrant officer, a veteran of the First Cavalry and its own disaster in Korea, came to me and said, "I know where you were today. I have been there. It won't be easy from now on. Be careful when you sleep." He was an alcoholic and when he talked to me that night, he was on his way to the one place that permitted him to continue functioning.

When the city returned to "friendly" control, and the North Vietnamese flag was taken down from the Buddha, I sat down and wrote to the command chaplain at Long Bhin, requesting a transfer to the First Cavalry Division. Within weeks, I switched places with an Episcopal Chaplain who had been with the First Cavalry for six months and was in need of rotation. Something about that day at the hospital showed me that war was not to be observed from hotel rooftops and that once contaminated by it you needed to stay in it. Even then, my unconscious urge was to stay on the side of danger–and not to come back just yet.

Twenty years later, when I was hospitalized for chest pains prior to coronary bypass surgery, I had received a shot of morphine one evening at about 9:30. I had been in considerable pain and had been more than significantly depressed emotionally. I fell asleep following the shot and woke up about two hours later. For the next hour or so, I was in two existences at the same time. I was fully aware that the room was in the Columbus, Georgia Medical Center, but the room was filled with the dead from the morgue in Nha Trang. The young dead man with the blue eyes still asked his questions and still looked up in astonishment. The young man with the clipboard still wandered aimlessly. In the midst of my panic, I knew I did not want another shot of any kind. I chose not to call nursing, not wanting further medication. My wife had left the hospital not long before, but I knew she was exhausted. I chose instead to call a nurse at the hospital where I worked. (Her husband was also a Vietnam veteran, so she understood war-related trauma.) I asked her to help to keep me in this present reality as long as she could and to keep me from slipping entirely, completely, totally, into that past reality. I told her if she had to leave the phone, that was okay, but she had to come back whenever she could. She did just that. For the next several hours, she remained in contact with me until I was able to let the room clear and my own integration took place once again.

This kind of experience was to happen in various forms for the next several years (with pain medication and without it). There were several forms of flashbacks, each with its own message and character. I still experience them in the emotional background of my mind, but they are no longer projected onto the present reality. I do not know if it will always be this way.[8]

NOTES

1. Lifton, Robert Jay. *Home from the War: Vietnam Veterans* (New York: Basic Books, 1973).

2. Shatan, Chaim F. "The Tattered Ego of Survivors," *Psychiatric Annals*, 12:11, November 1982), pp. 103ff.

3. American Psychiatric Association's *Diagnostic and Statistical Manual of Mental Disorders*, Third Edition, Revised (Washington, D.C.: American Psychiatric Association, 1987).

4. Fromm, Erich. *Sane Society* (New York: Rinehart & Company, 1955) p. 119.

5. van der Kolk, Bessel. *Psychological Trauma* (Washington, D.C.: American Psychiatric Press, 1987), p. 2.

6. Langer, L.L. *The Holocaust and the Literary Imagination* (New Haven: Yale University Press, 1975) p. 124.

7. Figley, Charles R., Ed. *Trauma and Its Wake* (New York: Brunner/Mazel, 1985), p. 296.

8. Two excellent books that serve as a good overview of this subject are:

Brende, Joel O. and Erwin R. Parson. *Vietnam Veterans: The Road to Recovery* (New York: Plenum Press, 1985).

Sonnenbert, Stephen M. et al. *The Trauma of War: Stress Recovery in Viet Nam Veterans* (Washington: American Psychiatric Press, 1985).

Chapter 2

The Results of Trauma

THE STORY OF CLYDE

When Clyde became aware that he had been watching the Weather Channel for about four hours, the numbness in his body was matched by the lack of feeling in his soul. He had been growing more and more aware that the numbness that enveloped him was now becoming impenetrable. Tonight, the eye of the TV screen projected its color and images toward his head like a laser beam, not really entering, but at least touching the outer surface and serving as some contact with a world beyond himself. When he thought of his passive state, he was aware that it was broken by a slow trickle of energy that enabled him to flip channels, making some form of contact with shades of different color and action once in a while. Yet he did not linger on the other channels very long, because staying there felt like being stuck and that needed to be avoided.

The dream had awakened him, and it was too awful to return to sleep. He chose to stay awake, but his being awake now had a different character to it. Not only must he stay awake, he needed to do two other things. He needed to allow that turbulent inner world that expressed itself in his dreams to slumber. In addition, he needed to stay keenly alert.

Suddenly, Clyde sat bolt upright and moved slowly toward the front door. After an hour, he returned to his seat in the den. He was drenched with sweat and was breathing heavily. He looked haggard and carried in his hand his old hunting knife in its well-oiled case. The weather patterns on TV had not changed much in the last hour or so, but Clyde was not really aware of any of it. He had now pulled his last round of "guard duty" for the night. It was not long before he heard his wife in the back of the house, and he went and put the morning coffee on, knowing that relative safety was now approaching with daylight. His nightly guard duty was over, and his day at work would be a relief from the night's routine.

At noon, Clyde had his secretary call his wife to tell her he would be working late and would not be home until about 11 p.m. He stayed in his office and stared at the walls until about 9 p.m., then went down to the river and sat with his back against an old oak tree and stared upstream for the next two hours. He walked into his home at 11:15 p.m., very aware that he had messed up another wedding anniversary. The flowers that he had sent by the florist sat on the dining room table, the card unopened. His pain was overwhelming when he opened a beer and picked up the channel changer. He heard his wife in the bedroom but could not bring himself to go back there. As he bathed himself in the light of the TV coming into the den's darkness, he felt the warfare inside himself subside. The alcohol and the hypnotic effect of the TV numbed him to a level that enabled him to not be in touch and to not care, if only for the moment. He was on guard duty again, and it was best not to feel.

THE STORY OF JANE

In another part of town, Jane left work at 5:30 p.m., and an hour later she was home to begin dinner. Today had been a routine day and she felt good about being in the kitchen at home, a relief from the phones and decisions of her day at work. Her husband, Tom, would be in at about 7 p.m. and they would have a quiet dinner together. As she absent-mindedly went through the day's mail, she suddenly felt very sad. She remembered the new person's question at work today about how far Jane lived from work. It came to her all of a sudden. Five miles from work and it takes an hour? The reality hit her. Day after day, she automatically made up new stories to cover this fact. Rolls had to be gotten across town. Cleaning needed to be picked up at the dry cleaners she preferred at the out-of-the way mall. But today it hit her. She never traveled down the direct street between home and work. The pain of that street was too much. It took too many days to recover and too much pain and energy to put it all back together whenever she went that way. It was far easier to take an hour getting home than to confront horror on a daily basis. Few others realized it, and her husband never mentioned her ritual avoidance. It was part of the unspoken pain.

DUNCAN'S JOURNEY

Clyde and Jane join Kate, Tony, Ann, and myself from Chapter 1 in this unfolding look at the results of trauma in people's lives. Within every parish and pastoral counseling center, people carry with them the pain of trauma. Some of that pain is so obvious that it overwhelms us when we see it ourselves. Most of it has become so subtle to others that it is difficult to fathom its depths. People who survive severe trauma become expert at avoidance and at hiding pain because it is constantly present and because it is so alien to those around them. Through their own interpretation of events, friends and loved ones, along with clergy and counselors, often misread the actions of traumatized people.

Not only are people directly affected by severe trauma, but those around them are likewise affected (and this always includes helpers at all levels of assistance). In the stories told here, we have taken a look at some of the pervasive features of trauma. As the "Story of Duncan" indicated, my own experiences with the results of traumata are both professional and personal. Perhaps sharing with you additional portions of my own journey will provide one useful way of looking at the many facets of traumata.

On the way to lunch one day, a new colleague of mine asked me how it had been possible for me to go into the military, especially during Vietnam. Anxious to enjoy lunch, I chose to sidestep the issue by saying it was too complex and perhaps too personal to be talked about over lunch. The question is not a new one, however. It is one I have dealt with for many years, and each time I or others raise it, different shades of light and darkness surround it. I have answered the question in many ways, and all my answers have been true, albeit perhaps very limited in each response. I know that my response, even at this point, will not be complete because my awareness of *the* answer is still unfolding. The response that I give now is not, in any sense, systematic. It is given on many levels, and I ask you to consider all parts of it.

Resigning as vicar of Trinity Episcopal Church in Bryan, Ohio, in the spring of 1966 to enter the U.S. Army as a chaplain was not a fully conscious choice. The week I went to discuss this with my bishop, his son joined the Marine Corps. Our discussion was not a rational one. Bishop Burroughs offered me a parish on the other side of the diocese, but we both knew that his offer was pro forma. Robert Nelson Burroughs, son of Bishop and Mrs. Nelson Burroughs, died in Vietnam on July 8, 1968. I was probably less than 50 miles from him when he died, though we never met. He was 23 when he died. Bishop Burroughs sent out a note to many of us, which in his own noble way said: "We are thankful to have had such a son and brother, and proud that he, like so many others, has given his life that men might be free."

In preparing to enter Trinity Cathedral in Cleveland for the opening service of the diocesan convention of 1969, a goodly number of my fellow clergy chose not to speak to me "out of conscience." An Army chaplain just back from Vietnam was, by their conviction of conscience, a persona non grata. I say this to illustrate the painful division that conscience has so very often created among us. The beginning of some healing came one night at the Norseman Lodge in Bethel, Maine, in the summer of 1976. A group of us from a National Training Laboratory Workshop sat in front of a fire and talked. A Jewish social worker from Cleveland and I shared a common view of the world for a brief moment. I had been a chaplain in Vietnam; he, along with a group of Jesuits, had chained himself to the gates of the American Embassy in Saigon. Because we had both "eyeballed" the depths of human hurt in Vietnam, we spoke a common language.

I was the seventh son—five of whom lived to adulthood—in a Scottish family in northern Maine. My four older brothers all served in the military. All were proud of their service, which was evidenced by their participation in the local Memorial Day parades. World War II saw Donald, John, and Hollis serve in the Navy; the Korean Conflict saw my oldest brother Donald return to the Navy and Bob, the fourth son, serve in the Army. When men from my parish were drafted to serve in Vietnam, I was—not surprisingly—drawn into the long march of men who went off to war.

To those who become connected to the collective unconscious in their daily lives, there are some places where you do not have to choose to be, where individual choice is secondary. In my own life, there are two such places: (1) in church, saying Mass with all the richness of historical trappings, joining with the whole company of heaven; and (2) in the field, marching in a column of soldiers that reaches back into history. I say this not to rationalize or justify any action. I say it because, from this historical vantage point, it seems to be most true. I have reflected often from theological, sociological, emotional, and psychological vantage points on why I chose to do what I did in 1966. Some of my conclusions are meaningful and, perhaps in another place, need to be written down. I am now over 50 years old, and the point from which I do my reflecting has so changed that I doubt I can ever again enter my mindset in 1966. I now live within the confines of those decisions, as my social worker friend from the Bethel conference in Maine no doubt lives with his. The decisions we made have shaped us and brought us to today.

As I stated in Chapter 1, my own trauma during the war began during the season of Tet in 1968. From there, I joined the First Cavalry Division and went to the northernmost section of Vietnam. From Camp Evans to Khe Shan to the Ah Shau Valley, up and down Route 1 from Landing Zones (LZs) Nancy, Sharon, and Betty, I served as Episcopal Chaplain to the division. Also, I was the battalion chaplain for the 8th Engineer Battalion, whose units were assigned to major units of the entire division.

I saw the war from many perspectives. From the hotel rooftop in Nha Trang to a foxhole in the dirt shared with men who froze in fear and terror at the thought of another artillery shell coming in from "out there." The shells did continue to come in, and with each one, a portion of who we were ceased to be alive to experience the terror. Instead, we dreamed dreams and talked of steak and sex and being home. The terror froze us solid. Before long, we each sat and ate C-ration fruitcake, ham, and lima beans, responding in slow motion when the next incoming round of artillery announced itself. On occasion, I was pinned down by our own exploding ammunition and fuel dumps. There seemed to be no let up, and we seemed to be trapped in Dante's *Inferno*. The shellings seemed to create a vivid color slide show of my own personal life. Brilliant scenes of historical still lifes filled my brain. I began to laugh and said aloud, "My life is flashing by! So this is how it happens!" The detachment and separations of trauma were, as I now see, taking shape in formidable ways.

Because of my office, not because of who I was, I sometimes ate in the generals' mess: rock lobster tail (not Maine), steak, wine, and a reading of the night-movie summary by the adjutant. The war of maps and the war from 5,000 feet were discussed with severe detachment by those whose job it was to be division staff. It is apparent now that each of us used great psychological warfare to keep the killing, the real war, at as safe a distance as we could create in our own way. Distance! Distance! Distance! A must for survival. Don't get close! It will suck you in and destroy you. This place sucks! (This motto of Vietnam said it well.) One day, a battalion commander said to me, "Chaplain, you don't think this place sucks, do you?" My response was immediate: "Think about it, sir. Have you noticed that all the flags on the compound fly toward the center of the base?" Without distancing ourselves, there would have been no survivors.

One day, we flew to the decks of the *U.S.S. Sanctuary*. The great white Navy hospital ship lay off the coast at a safe distance, cradling in her hold and sterile sheets those who had been badly wounded just hours before. I was overwhelmed by the cleanliness of the ship. White walls, white sheets, white uniforms. Everywhere, there was a brilliant, brilliant white. I could not remember when I had put on my fatigues, I simply wore them. Mud and my flesh were a fusion now, as they were with all of us who had flown out that afternoon. We visited our wounded. I prayed. The colonel handed out Purple Hearts. We talked with a young, proud officer who was a West Pointer. He had lost his leg in surgery hours before, and he wept when talking with us. He died shortly after from throwing a fat embolism. We went into the Officers' Mess and ate from china and were served by stewards from the Philippines. I do not recall what I ate, but I was sick for days afterward. We flew back to our land position and it felt comfortable. We knew the limits at our base. We knew how to survive in these surroundings. We had created the right distance. The hospital ship was too foreign and unknown. It created a sharp dissonance deep within each of us.

Those who have said that John Wayne died in Vietnam were right. John Wayne won his fame by creating distance between war and the American public. He told the American public what they wanted to believe about combat and about not dying. One of the most vivid dreams I have ever had was in black and white, like an old movie.

While I normally dream in color, this was in that grainy black-and-white that conveyed such poignant depth of meaning. I stood at the entrance of my tent at battalion headquarters. Many of the men from the unit stood in a loose circle around a pit that had been dug at the center of the battalion. An acute and mysterious silence permeated the whole scene. A small bulldozer moved slowly and began to fill the gaping hole. I heard someone ask, "What are they doing?" "They're burying Christ," came the reply. I stood at the door of my tent and watched, immobile and without feeling.

Our flight left Vietnam and arrived in California one hour before we "left" Vietnam, thanks to time-zone changes. Within hours, our families were united; within a matter of weeks, I was back in the "real" Army. I was assigned as Staff Chaplain for Ireland Army Hospital at Fort Knox, Kentucky. Deep inside, I knew that this was not right. I asked for an alternative assignment. It was denied. They said, "With all the dependents in this area, we need someone who can do emergency infant baptisms. The assignment is yours." Oh, to have been Baptist! I thought.

I went into my office and stared at the walls for months. When they talked about the dying children, they had not mentioned that there were masses of beds filled with dying and healing soldiers home from Vietnam. My soul, mind, and body were cold and numb. I woke up many mornings on the floor of my bedroom, having heard the tanks on the ranges firing during the night. After several months, my wife's compassionate intervention and a wise senior chaplain moved me to a training unit. With mud and fatigues, I could muster a pretense at being alive.

During this time, the Archdeacon of my diocese invited me to return to the Diocese of Ohio. I spent a bit of time looking at the parish, a small college-town church in a progressive community. Several weeks later, the Senior Warden of the parish called and invited me to come and be their rector. With almost no hesitation, I thanked him and said no. I knew deep within that my Vietnam experiences had changed me too much to be a rector in a college town and pretend that all was well. I did not know how to say that then, but I now know that unresolved feelings about death and shame and war do not make a good foundation for parish ministry. At that moment,

I needed to remain with the company of those who had known what I had known.

Two years later, I was on an airplane flying west from Louisville to Kansas City, when we lost an engine on takeoff and had to dump fuel up north and land again. After that incident, it was on to San Francisco, Alaska, Japan, and then Vietnam once again. They were taking ground fire in Ton San Nhut, where we were to land, so we landed in Cam Rhan Bay, which I had watched recede into the west when I had flown out two years before. I have often been asked how I was able to return to Vietnam. I have replied straight out, "I was sober the first time in."

I flew on to Red Beach, where I spent the next year doing all I could to stay numb, ultra-distant, and out of harm's way. A small group of us on our second and third tours huddled together in a loving, protective enclave and survived. Outside my family, I have never known such care and love. There was a mutual protection and respect of the wounds that each one of us shared. Not that we "typical" males acknowledged what was happening; but happen it did. Except for a few brief attempts shortly after our return to the U.S., none of us has shared the bond we had during the war. This troubled me often, and I could not understand why the closeness we shared disappeared. Today, I realize that closeness was inevitably linked to a very painful place and time. To try to recreate that experience in a world that could not know or see our pain did not seem possible. Therefore, it did not seem okay to continue this relationship in a world that, from every angle, was forcing us to forget the past. We were also growing more and more convinced that perhaps forgetting was the only way to go.

Fort Campbell in Kentucky was my duty station following my return from this second tour in Vietnam. The 101st Airborne Division returned to Fort Campbell just as broken and as destroyed by the war as the rest of us. My task during my two years at this assignment was to attempt to deal with some of the brokenness by following official Army doctrine, which was to forget. To forget Vietnam. To forget the pain of combat. To forget the realities of what just had been. "Rendezvous with Destiny," the old World War II motto of the 101st Airborne Division, was resurrected and all eyes were turned once again to heroic future battles that were to be fought in Europe or the great deserts.

Some of us sat in field tents sipping Kentucky bourbon and quietly weeping with each other when we experienced communal flashbacks in the night. Vietnam was still deep within us and within the division, in spite of the new coats of paint on the surrounding walls and the Army's attempts to create new visions of the future.

The only way the military had to mourn was to bury its dead with some degree of dignity. During my tour at Fort Knox, and later at Fort Campbell, much of my duty was spent in notifying families of deaths and helping them with the details of burying their dead. I assisted in funeral services from mountain tops in Virginia to tobacco fields in South Carolina and from Louisville to the deep valleys of Tennessee. Taps were sounded and rifles were fired in salute. Flags were presented to the families to say symbolically what words themselves could not say. It was an era when symbols were ridiculed, and yet most of what was said at such times could only be said in symbolic ways.

The war was over for most of us, and the joy of that fact kept us protected for awhile. Planning for the future took over, along with some celebration for being alive and having survived. Life was rigid and unreal, but it was there nonetheless and "time would heal all wounds." The terrifying dreams in the night were considered a temporary price to pay. Surely, they would not last forever. Being glad to be home made up for the emotional strangeness that prevailed. The increased emotional distance and growing emotional withdrawal from all that was personal and that had past meaning seemed to help us appear normal. This normality was also played out by the excitement of being home, at least for some of us. In the midst of this time, my youngest brother Bob died in northern Maine. I flew home in March into the cold and blizzard conditions and tried to say farewell. We said our clumsy good-byes, but we could not bury him because of the blizzard. They waited until spring. As I flew home, I realized that death had in many ways taken over the design of my psychic state during the past five years, and the momentum to live grew slower and slower.

In June of 1974, my family and I left Kentucky and moved to Fort Hamilton in New York. I spent a year at the Army Chaplains' School, and during that time did a year of graduate work at Long Island University in downtown Brooklyn. For the first time since 1962, I was not on pastoral duty and, thus, not continuously on call. Once again, I was with a close group of good friends. The year was in many ways a reprieve. I did well at both schools. A number of us refused to take the final physical training test at the Chaplains' School. It was in its own way a symbolic rebellion against the status quo.

Seven months after being assigned to Fort Benning in Georgia ("the Home of the Infantry"), I walked into a private psychiatric hospital as a voluntary inpatient. Numb, depressed, and without hope or meaning, I could not march one more step. The hospital was notable for its compassion and professionalism. The kindness of the staff supplemented the prolonged support I had for so long received from my wife and children. For six weeks, I participated in a wide range of therapies: individual, chemical, group, intensive group, family, couples, and recreational. Not once was Vietnam considered a significant contributing factor. The trauma of war, of death, of prolonged horror was never considered as a significant part of what was being played out in my life.

This is not said in judgment. It is said to convey the fact that trauma has only just recently been considered significant in terms of the psychic, spiritual, and physical damage that it causes. From the mental-health perspective of just a little over a decade ago, a person's reaction to trauma was the result of conditions that existed prior to the trauma. The trauma was not considered significant, only the psychic substructure that existed prior to the trauma. Translated, this says, in part: if you suffer seriously from the results of trauma, there was something wrong with you prior to the trauma; that defective part of you needs to be corrected. In addition to the mental-health perspective, there was the response of a local clergyperson–when my wife called and asked for communion to be brought to the hospital–"I really don't have much to do with that place, but if you insist . . ."

I left the Army in 1978. I resigned, knowing that healing for myself and for my family needed to take place outside the military. The Army, like so many institutions, was dysfunctional in the sense that it was filled with mixed messages: "We care for our own" and "Take this hill that we will give back to the enemy next week–and die trying."

In 1982, having had coronary bypass surgery the year before, I spent two months as an inpatient at the Tuskegee Veterans' Administration (VA) Hospital, attempting to deal with the ongoing inner struggle of Vietnam. This seemed to be the place to do it. With few exceptions, however, the staff was not prepared to deal with the trauma of my life. Giving me asylum and a structure within which to work out my own struggle with fear and trembling seemed to have been sufficient for them. It was during this period that my second-youngest brother, Hollis, died. I was unable to return to Maine at that point to say good-bye. On occasion, I drive to the nearest VA cemetery and place flowers for both of my brothers. This simple bit of ritualistic contact is very meaningful to me.

Following that period, and until recently, I have led, been a part of, and worked with a Vietnam Veterans Support and Therapy Group for my own benefit and for the support and therapy of other group members. This group has helped form much of what I know about using group therapy to heal from trauma.

CLINICAL DIAGNOSIS OF POST-TRAUMATIC STRESS DISORDER

Turning now from personal accounts of the effects of trauma, it is important that we place them in clinical perspective. PTSD–the clinical diagnosis that originated as the result of soldiers' experiences in the Vietnam War and that is now applied to a wide range of traumatic events–was first defined as a disorder by the American Psychiatric Association in 1980. The following is the most current criteria for diagnosing PTSD, taken from the American Psychiatric Association's 1987 revised third edition of the *Diagnostic and Statistical Manual of Mental Disorders* (DSM III-R).[1]

DIAGNOSTIC CRITERIA FOR 309.89 POST-TRAUMATIC STRESS DISORDER

A. The person has experienced an event that is outside the range of usual human experience and that would be markedly distressing to almost anyone, e.g., serious threat to one's life or physical integrity, serious threat or harm to one's children, spouse, or other close relatives and friends; sudden destruction of one's home or community; or seeing another person who has recently been, or is being seriously injured or killed as the result of an accident or physical violence.

B. The traumatic event is persistently reexperienced in at least one of the following ways:

1. recurrent and intrusive distressing recollections of the event (in young children, repetitive play in which themes or aspects of the trauma are expressed)
2. recurrent distressing dreams of the event
3. sudden acting or feeling as if the traumatic event were recurring (includes a sense of reliving the experience, illusions, hallucinations, and dissociative (flashback) episodes, even those that occur upon awakening or when intoxicated)
4. intense psychological distress at exposure to events that symbolize or resemble an aspect of the traumatic event, including anniversaries of the trauma

C. Persistent avoidance of stimuli associated with the trauma or numbing of general responsiveness (not present before the trauma), as indicated by at least three of the following:

1. efforts to avoid thoughts or feelings associated with the trauma
2. efforts to avoid activities or situations that arouse recollections of the trauma
3. inability to recall an important aspect of the trauma (psychogenic amnesia)
4. markedly diminished interest in significant activities (in young children loss of recently acquired developmental skills such as toilet training or language skills)
5. feelings of detachment or estrangement from others
6. restricted range of affect, e.g., unable to have loving feelings
7. sense of foreshortened future, e.g., does not expect to have a career, marriage, or children, or a long life

D. Persistent symptoms of increased arousal (not present before the trauma, as indicated by at least two of the following:

1. difficulty falling or staying asleep
2. irritability or outbursts of anger
3. difficulty concentrating
4. hypervigilance
5. exaggerated startle response
6. physiologic reactivity upon exposure to events that symbolize or resemble an aspect of the traumatic event (e.g., woman who was raped in an elevator breaks out in a sweat when entering any elevator)

In the unemotional tone of the technical manual, we have a summary of only the psychological effects of severe trauma in the lives of persons who have experienced it. Clergy, families, and pastoral counselors know that the effects of PTSD are much more pervasive. They reach into every facet of human living. At this point, however, let us look at the psychological effects of PTSD outlined in the above quotation.

The reality of PTSD is that the traumatic event is persistently reexperienced. This is one of the most difficult symptoms to understand. To see that which is not there is a classic symptom of insanity (the one that is most feared, in fact). "I'm losing my mind!" is the first thought of many who begin to "see" again that which was lived in the midst of trauma. To see again. To relive. To reexperience in the form of "recurrent and intrusive distressing recollections of the event." To know that past event once again in "recurrent distressing dreams." This, perhaps, we can understand. But "feeling as if the traumatic event were recurring," even when one is fully awake and sober, crosses over into a different realm of experience not ordinarily known to most people. Those who care for, and minister to, victims of severe trauma need to understand that the rape victim, for instance, repeatedly experiences the assault in all aspects of all senses. For a victim to remember a rape that happened ten years ago is one thing. To remember it with severe vaginal pain ten years later is a different level of reality. To remember being shot at ten years ago is one thing. To remember it with loss of bowel control ten years later is a different level of reality. To remember holding a dying child fifteen years ago is one thing. To remember holding a dying child and smell the rancid fever and see the eyes of helplessness is a different level of reality. To actually see and experience over and over and over again the image of a dying wife at the burning window–not just remembering the image–is a different level of reality.

The awful experience of being frozen within the horrific trauma exists outside that which we intellectually call the ego. The experience is, quite simply, too awful to invite in and make it a part of who we are. It must remain foreign, outside, and unintegrated. Our best judgment continually pushes us to reject it: "It never was! It does not exist! It does not belong to me! It never did happen!" These thoughts conflict with self-perception: "It is me. It is mine. It is my experience. It happened in my life." This is the status of the embattled ego, the besieged self. The denial of our normal reality conflicts with the denial of the horrific reality, thus triggering flashbacks. In very simple, non-technical terms, flashbacks are images so repugnant to our sense of self that we project them onto the world "out there." We cannot tolerate seeing these images in our inner life, as a part of who we are. They must be seen out there–in reality–apart from who we are. We objectify them to the point that they take on a life of their own, albeit at a safe distance from our own egos.

The initial reaction of helpers, clergy, and others to those who experience flashbacks is to attempt to demythologize the experience for themselves and to help alleviate the pain of the sufferers. Responses such as "Time heals all wounds," "This will soon be behind you," and "It's all in your mind" are obviously very inadequate responses. When dealing with the effects of horrific trauma, they are not only not helpful, they will also tend to *increase* the effects of the trauma in the life of the person.

THE STORY OF ALICE

Alice sat in the restaurant saying very little that evening. Eye contact was made only when absolutely necessary. She focused on Tim's hand with great intensity. She watched the raised blue veins, the gold ring worn smooth by the years. She watched droplets of water run down the outside of the water glass at a slow irregular pace. She knew that if anyone looked, they would see her heart pounding beneath her pink dress. Her hands were moist as she cut her steak with great deliberation. Tim had asked her a question and was waiting for the answer. She looked at him with as quick and unfocused a look as she could manage. She was frozen now with fear and looked away. In place of Tim's normally soft and loving face, she saw the face of the bank robber, Jan. The face was filled with inhuman cruelty, and his eyes projected sadistic terror. Years of work enabled Alice to freeze her thoughts and to hold on to two realities at the same time: the reality of *now* (with Tim, in the restaurant) and the reality of *then* (with Jan, in that airless bank vault eight years ago today). She tasted blood now as she bit her lip to retain control. It would pass; that was the fact that she now knew after years of experience. But why tonight? Why now? Why here in this place?

Later, as Alice worked in her support group, she pieced together the mini-bits of experience that had triggered the events of the evening in the restaurant with Tim. The trip to the bank today to put the new will into the safety deposit box; her date with Tim; the fact that Tim had spoken harshly to her on the way into the city. These were relatively minor events, yet they created a gestalt that brought Jan's face into sharp focus for a minute of sheer horror in the midst of what should have been a relaxing evening.

In the life of the trauma victim, experiences such as these are commonplace. Dreams, super-intense recollections, flashbacks, and dissociative experiences continue for years. Usually, they are lived out in secret. To deal with the intrusive nature of the trauma, the trauma victim commits to, in the words of DSM III-R, a "persistent avoidance of stimuli associated with the trauma." At one level of avoidance, Jane (at the beginning of this chapter) avoided a certain street. For the most part, this was relatively simple–go around it and go home another way. Her three-year-old daughter had been killed on that street in a car accident while Jane was driving. Jane had held her little girl on the way to the hospital, where she later died. Jane goes to great lengths to avoid reexperiencing the sounds of grating metal and screams of horror and the feeling of that limp body in her arms on the way to the hospital.

In Jane's home, there are no photographs or other traces of her daughter. It as if the child never existed. This is the other level of avoidance. Jane works at keeping her memory to the absolute minimum. Her husband, to manage his own pain, contributes to the avoidance routine. They both attempt to live as though their daughter had never been born. To maintain this posture, they must stay away from each other. To keep emotionally shut down, Jane and her husband must dance the dance of distance and stay numb to themselves and to each other. Eating and loving are routine events done without feeling or emotion and certainly without passion. Jane is into saving the whales and her husband is into fighting a toxic waste dump. These are excellent causes, and they help the couple focus much of who they are "out there," beyond the confines of their own pain. They attended church until six months ago, when they were both angered by new plans to remodel the parish hall. They have not talked to anyone about their anger.

THE STORY OF LLOYD

Lloyd always drinks mountain water and eats rabbit three times a week. He has lived with the back of his cabin door up against the mountain for the past six years. From his front door, he can see down into the valley for miles, until it turns into a blue haze. He sleeps from about 8 a.m. to 3 p.m. daily. The rest of the time, he is alert and watches. He goes into the village once a month for coffee and tobacco and to pick up his 10 percent disability check from the VA. He stands at the counter in the drugstore where he buys his pipe tobacco. He talks to the older woman at the register for about five minutes each month. This is the extent of his human contact. His conversation is usually about the MIAs and POWs in Vietnam. He says he thinks about them all the time. One day, he will fail to come for his check, and his war will be over.

THE STORY OF MARIA

Maria had been in therapy for about two years and had had a number of significant hospitalizations. She had been in both private and public hospitals, having repeatedly attempted suicide. At the time I saw her, she had been performing self-mutilation. Razor blades were her instruments of choice. Her fascination with bleeding and cutting was consuming much of her energy when I began seeing her. In the case history I received from her therapist, no known reason for the mutilation was indicated. Psychological testing and projective drawings all pointed toward significant trauma in her early life, but this was clearly denied by Maria. The trauma she did acknowledge involved a marriage that terminated with Maria losing custody of her child. Yet the pattern of her mutilation and the pattern of the projective drawings and testing all pointed toward early trauma, and very likely incest. She noted significant periods of lost time in her daily activity. She would "lose the razor blades" and really not know where they were. She would get up at night and cook, surprised to find the meals the next morning. She was an only child, but she was very alienated from both parents. In dealing with anger toward her present husband, she began to focus on her father's inappropriate behavior. He had always treated her as his confidante, sharing with her his anger and fear that her mother had been unfaithful. In therapy, Maria was able to become angry, and she realized that it was her relationship with her father that had troubled her. Her father's level of intimacy with her, she felt, had been inappropriate.

During one period of hospitalization, Maria began having frightening dreams of her father. She found this odd, having never been frightened of her father before. She said that she was always able to manipulate him with ease and that he had never been a threat to her. At this point, she began hypnotherapy. During this work, she acknowledged a part of her that had not come out in therapy. She spoke of this part of herself as "very dark and filled with pain." She said that this was the part of herself that always knew where the razor blades were. This was the part of her who did the cutting.

Following several months of continuing therapy, and about four sessions of hypnotherapy, Maria was able to reconstruct a scene during which her father had raped her when she was twelve years of age. She was given permission during the hypnotherapy to remember or not remember when she left the trance state, since it was her choice to continue the "not knowing" or to remember. As soon as she came out of the trance state, she sat bolt upright and said: "He did it! He raped me on the living room couch." It has taken a great deal more work, but the connection of the mutilations and the incest are begin-

ning to take place, with a significant decrease in the number of cut-
tings.

The ability of Maria to "forget" in order to survive is important to
note. As described in DSM III-R, this "inability to recall an important
aspect of the trauma (psychogenic amnesia)" is, I believe, a concept
with very important theological and pastoral considerations. For the
moment, we need to be in touch with the fact that amnesia about
details of trauma and whole traumatic events does indeed exist. On
the surface, this means that what people present in pastoral counseling, in therapy, or in pastoral care settings may not be the whole story.
We are sensitive to facts being guarded and unshared because of
shame or other forms of emotional pain, but that is not what we are
dealing with here. We are talking about details of trauma and whole
traumatic events that are *not consciously remembered*. They do not
exist in the conscious memory at the present time. They are *not
remembered*. The details are not available. Maria did not share the
details of her father's raping her because she felt emotional shame or
fear of blame. She did not share it in therapy *because she did not
remember it*. Instead, she reenacted it over and over again, complete
with bleeding and denial of pain. Her rage at being raped could not,
in her childlike frame of mind, be directed at her father. It was instead
held at arm's length, unintegrated and alien to her. Instead of attacking
her father, years later she began to attack herself, not knowing the
source of her rage. As her anger took on a less-than-alien nature, she
was able to acknowledge that the rage did not need to be self-directed.
Her anger could then be directed outward, in an adult-to-adult rage
toward her father.

THE LEGACY OF TRAUMA

In psychological terms, a victim of severe trauma persistently re-
experiences the trauma in distressing dreams of the event. The
dreams often have a historical character of reality in that they occur
again and again. Victims not only dream, they reexperience when
conscious and sober or when under the influence of alcohol or drugs.
The reexperiencing is not just remembering, it is as though the event
were recurring in illusions, and dissociative episodes. In terms of

behavior, we see victims of trauma becoming detached from life and intimacy, with a limited range of feelings. Events that recall the trauma are avoided, as are places or events that activate the victim's basic hypervigilance or exaggerated startle response. Rage, in its myriad forms, is part of the legacy of trauma in the lives of victims.

LOSSES AND SEPARATIONS

In addition to the psychological effects of trauma, there are many other consequences, including spiritual losses. These spiritual losses of trauma are varied and touch the very core of the victim. They include, but certainly are not limited to, loss of trust, loss of faith, loss of innocence, loss of hope, loss of purpose, loss of meaning, and loss of joy.

"I watched myself being beaten from across the room. I felt no pain, only overwhelming sadness, and I wondered why I was alive." On first reading, this statement sounds very strange indeed. Yet it is a phrase I have heard innumerable times in the course of psychotherapy with victims of abuse. At the moment when the pain is most severe, there is that natural separation of *body* and *self*. The body remains, receiving the continued abuse, while the self moves out of harm's way and is the silent observer. The radical split that occurs at this moment then becomes the means for future survival from escalating abuse. This experience is difficult to explain to persons who have never known it. To victims of abuse and trauma, there is no need for explanation; it is the awful rescue from pain.

The following poem by Anne Sexton (entitled "Courage") is a glimpse into the pain following separation from self and others.

It is in the small things we see it.
The child's first step,
as awesome as an earthquake.
The first time you rode a bike,
wallowing up the sidewalk.
The first spanking when your heart
went on a journey all alone.
When they called you crybaby

or poor or fatty or crazy
and made you into an alien,
and you drank their acid
and concealed it.

Later,
if you faced the death of bombs and bullets
you did not do it with a banner,
you did it with only a hat to
cover your heart.
You did not fondle the weakness inside you
though it was there.
Your courage was a small coal
that you kept swallowing.
If your buddy saved you
and died himself in so doing,
then his courage was not courage,
it was love; love as simple as shaving soap.

Later,
if you have endured a great despair,
then you did it alone,
getting a transfusion from the fire,
picking the scabs off your heart,
then wringing it out like a sock.
Next, my kinsman, you powdered your sorrow,
and you gave it a back rub
and then you covered it with a blanket
and after it had slept a while
it woke to the wings of the roses
and was transformed.

Later,
when you face old age and its natural conclusion
your courage will still be shown in the little ways,
each spring will be a sword you'll sharpen,
those you love will live in a fever of love,
and you'll bargain with the calendar

and at the last moment
when death opens the back door
you'll put on your carpet slippers
and stride out.[2]

For the victims of severe trauma, the separation goes way beyond a time "when your heart went on a journey all alone." Beyond that space, there is that extra space where pain indeed has "made you into an alien, and you drank their acid and concealed it."

The traumata-inflicted existential separation from self and others creates a spiritual despair that lingers long after the physical or emotional pain has begun to heal. The self retreats into the recesses of the inner world until life is seen from way back there, down long tunnels of darkness where pass only shadows of life at the entrance. Connections and relationships are heard about, not experienced. Relationships and closeness are mimicked, not lived. Living is that which is played off of others, not that which flows from the center of being.

It is at this secret inner place that traumata have their severe power of destruction. Alienation from self and others is not confined to only certain forms of traumata; it is universal, flowing from all severe traumata.

SPIRITUAL EFFECTS

In the clinical vignettes in this chapter, we have looked at trauma affecting lives to the point where persons "left their bodies to survive," where people projected the faces of inflictors of trauma onto the faces of loved ones. We have seen how past trauma can be relived in this moment of time over and over again. We have seen how the effects of traumata can cause the reaching out for emotional connection to cease and how relationships can be discontinued in order to avoid the pain. We then ask, How can a viable spiritual life exist in the midst of all this? How can a connection with God be established in the midst of this radical separation? How can evil be seen as separate from goodness and vice versa?

This is not just the loss of innocence that some writers on the nature of trauma describe. The loss of innocence is when you learn your father cheated on his income tax. It is not when he beats you, breaking your bones, and then forces you to lie to the emergency room physician to cover up his violence. The loss of innocence is when your boyfriend or girlfriend goes out with another. It is not when your mother forces you to have sex with her friends for their pleasure and her profit. This level of trauma goes well beyond the loss of innocence. Once, I met with a committee that asked me to talk about my time in Vietnam. After I had said a few things, a member of the committee said: "I'm sure the Vietnam experience was your loss of innocence." My anger and hurt kept me from telling him that I had lost my innocence long before Vietnam. In Vietnam, I radically questioned the very existence of God and His purported goodness. This was way beyond the loss of innocence. In the Apocryphal Book of Sirach, we find this admonition:

> Son, if you are going to serve the Lord, be prepared for times when you will be put to the test. Be sincere and determined. Keep calm when trouble comes. Stay with the Lord; never abandon him, and you will be prosperous at the end of your days. Accept what happens to you . . .
>
> Think back to the ancient generations and consider this: has the Lord ever disappointed anyone who put his hope in him? Has the Lord ever abandoned anyone who held him in constant reverence? . . . the Lord is kind and merciful; he forgives our sins and keeps us safe in time of trouble. But those who lose their nerve are doomed–all those sinners who try to have it both ways. Doom is sure to come for those who lose their courage; they have no faith, and so they have no protection. Doom is sure to come for those who lose hope. What will they do when the Lord comes to judge them? (2:1-18, GNB)

". . . [T]hose who lose their nerve are doomed. . . . Doom is sure to come for those who lose their courage . . . Doom is sure to come for those who lose hope." These words pinpoint how serious traumata wipe out nerve, courage, and hope. Humankind has limits (our magnificent folklore to the contrary). Men cry out in agony when they die. Children trust and lose hope. Women love and are violently abused. Men extend the open palm and have their arm cut off. The spiritual crisis aroused by horrific traumata is universal: hope is removed and doom is put in its place.

PHYSICAL EFFECTS

The physical effects of horrific traumata are great. The significant work that has been done in recent years on the nature and effects of stress on the human body can, no doubt, be applied to victims of horrific traumata. Trauma victims experience any and all stress-related illnesses, and no doubt at levels beyond the average population. In addition, trauma has a significant contributing factor to any and all illnesses. Beyond this, the physical effects of serious traumata are legion. Much more research needs to be done. For the research to be done with relevance, however, the old mind/body split that plagues so much medical research needs to be overcome. The intuition and sensitivity of the pastor, chaplain, and pastoral counselor will at this point make more connections than objective medical research can make. We need to remember that this does in no way make physical effects less true. The bottom line for all professionals to note is that horrific traumata in the lives of persons will compromise them at many and varied physical levels for greatly extended periods of time.

NOTES

1. American Psychiatric Association: *Diagnostic and Statistical Manual of Mental Disorders*, Third Edition, Revised (Washington, D.C.: American Psychiatric Association, 1987).
2. Sexton, Anne. "Courage," *The Awful Rowing Toward God.* (Boston: Houghton Mifflin, 1975), p. 15ff.

Chapter 3

Trauma Delayed

It is time for our truth.
It feels right.
The classical Greeks knew it all along.
(The nature of man is best known
by considering nature itself).
It took Ulysses twenty years
to return from the wars
and put his house in order.
It's taken twenty years
to get from the Gulf of Tonkin Incident
to be here and now.
And it's taken twenty years
for this country to raise its children
to be the average age
of the college student to whom
the subject of Vietnam is addressed
and to whom the next war
seems ready to be served.

–Steve Mason
Jonny's Song: Poetry of a Vietnam Veteran[1]

MEMORY AND THE NOW

We are a people of memory. Our Judeo-Christian heritage is a spiritual way of life that claims the power of memory: The God of Abraham, Sara, Isaac, and Jacob; the God of Ruth and Miriam; and

Jesus' bidding to "This do in remembrance of Me." We demand that
our history--our memory--shape and mold our present and future.
Within this context, memory is never static. The Passover question
"Why is this night different?" is asked not only of the holy night of
deliverance but also of this night of today. Why are that night, this
night, and our future nights so very special? The Christian Eucharist
is a time warp beyond what any science fiction writer could comprehend. The Eucharist is first and foremost a mystical bringing together
of that night of the Last Supper, this moment, and the hope of the
heavenly banquet-all in one timeless moment set always within the
context of our present moment. To live in the Now-mystically beyond
the confines of time-is to bring the reality of the past, the special
quality of the present, and the ever-present hope of the future into the
Now. Time does not stand still; rather, it is no more.

In the Now, the confines of chronological time are no more, and we
are caught up in that which was, is, and will be. This is the language
of the mystic. Mystics speak the language of timelessness. The victims of trauma also speak the language of timelessness. The ecstatic
and the horrific both eradicate time as we know it. In dealing with
both the mystic and the victim of trauma, we too often insist on the
rigidity of linear time. We too often insist that time be as we have once
defined it, that the future be as we once hoped it to be, and that the
present be uncluttered by anything beyond our definition of it.

Our unconscious cannot tell time. Our core self cannot tell time.
Our essence is timeless. Our soul, our psyche, has meaning beyond
the confines of time. Time has meaning only in that it orders our days
and gives boundaries and structure to our living. But once we insist
that time must define either our mystical sense of timelessness or our
experience of the horrific, we attempt to define a reality in terms of
clock time. However, timelessness and horrific trauma are two separate ways of experiencing reality.

TIMELESSNESS AND THE PRESENT MOMENT

To come to an understanding of the timelessness of the unconscious, the concept of a linear time perspective must be set aside. To
insist that "that was in the past, you must now put it in historical
perspective" is to insist that the present experiential reality of the past

is not so. We are not dealing with memory, per se, in this context. Memory, as we commonly understand it, is to call into the present some intellectual understanding of what has been. Perhaps it will even be called into the present with some degree of emotion and affective recall. To stand in the middle of Arlington National Cemetery is an overwhelming experience for most people, regardless of whether or not they served in the military. To stand on The Mall in Washington, with all of its history, is to experience some sense of timelessness. To stand in the shadow of the chimneys at Dachau must cause horrified chills to run up the spine. Yet all this is only a hint of what victims of trauma know in the reexperiencing of that trauma. The pastor, the chaplain, and the pastoral counselor need to reach deep within their own spiritual experience and understanding in order to relate to the trauma victim's present experience. A radical breaking out of the confines of our ordinary understanding of time is an absolute necessity in order to begin to comprehend the trauma victim's reexperiencing of *present* pain. A trauma victim tells time differently. She experiences time differently. She knows time is measured differently than by clocks and calendars.

What has been known for centuries was relearned with great clarity following the Vietnam War. Serious trauma is dealt with long after the fact. The news of the San Francisco earthquake in 1989, just prior to the World Series game, gave us reports that there were people alive in the sandwiched sections of roadway where the upper level dropped onto the bottom layer. They were there–wounded and waiting with those who had already been dead for more than 16 hours. Over the years, victims come to deal with their emotional trauma over and over again. In moments of great stress, or under conditions that are similar to the initial trauma, victims will relive their suffering many times over.

Popular psychology and many self-help groups have emphasized, with much success, the need to live and function in the present. This is indeed a sound therapeutic principle. Often, however, these ideas do not take into account the dynamic of serious trauma. Telling a trauma victim to "live in the present" is useful to an extent. Flashbacks, however, are present material and not past memories. The intrusion of the past–with all its emotional power–into the present moment is not a conscious choice. The victim does not dredge this material up to screen out the present moment. It arrives full-blown in the present moment because the similarity of the present moment calls it into being. The unintegrated past is not a part of the ego; it is ego-alien, not belonging to the moment. The unintegrated past intrudes with its own alien power and dynamic, laying claim to the present when the ego is in a position of helplessness and powerlessness-not unlike that moment in history when the trauma began. The body and its autonomic nervous system are as responsive in the present moment as they were when they had to respond to survive.

PAST INTO PRESENT—THE INTRUSION OF TRAUMA

The "Post" in Post-Traumatic Stress Disorder means just that. The hyper-alertness, the fear, the anxiety, the sweating, the psychic numbing, the emotional distancing in the present moment are all the direct result of that which happened in the past. In the most simplistic terms, the trauma is too great, too alien, and too powerful to be incorporated into the reality of who the person is. The trauma sits there until it is driven into the present moment to be dealt with once again. It comes in many forms. At times, it is a massive eruption, and at other times it moves in silently over an extended period of time until it has once again overtaken the present moment with all its fury.

Victims of trauma have much difficulty understanding what is going on when they are revisited by trauma out of their past. To most of them, this is the closest thing to being insane. They see, they hear, they smell, they taste, they feel the past. To experience what is not there is the classic sign of mental illness. When you see what others do not see, when you smell what others do not smell, when you hear what others do not hear, the conclusion you reach is that you must be mentally ill. It is often at this point that the victim ceases to talk about what is happening. To share this bizarre experience is too risky. This, of course, enhances the withdrawal and the distancing from others. At this point, clergy and other helpers need to be prepared to risk moving closer and asking pointed, direct questions. It is appropriate to ask what is going on, what is being experienced. If trauma is known to have happened, direct questions about the present activity of the trauma need to be asked. A good rule of thumb to use is whether that which is seen, heard, felt, tasted, etc., is historical; if it is, then it is without doubt related to the nature of the past trauma. It does not have to be an exact replay of past events, but it will contain historical material from the rape, combat, incest, natural disaster, or whatever was the source of the trauma.

Traumatized people will often recount events from their past with a detached monotone, without emotion. They will end their story by saying, "But that is all in the past, and I don't let it bother me now." They will deny that the trauma has present impact. The trauma is thus kept at bay. They live their lives in "quiet desperation," in significant distance from others. They numb their emotions and avoid at all costs anything that might trigger memories of the traumatic event. Shutting down, and staying that way, requires most of their energy. The lid must be kept on no matter what. Rage and anger are often misdirected "out there," at whatever and whoever happens by–the little old lady in the slow-moving vehicle, the teenager with the long hair, or the government. In these ways, the trauma has its own remote action. It is seldom direct, but it has a daily effect on the quality of life of the people involved. It affects mood, feelings, actions, and, above all, relationships, but it is never dealt with. Its place is just beyond the range of daily activity.

Physically, emotionally, and spiritually the old moment is relived, not just remembered. The unconscious cannot tell time, and when it projects the ego-alien material onto the present moment, the time is both *then and now*. During some of these instances, the present is dimmed to the point where it is actually lost for periods of time. This is not a loss of reality, as is experienced in certain forms of mental illness. Rather, it is an experience of being captured by a past reality come to life in the present moment.

We know the reality of a timeless unconscious by the content of our dreams. Our own experience in dreaming is such that in our dream life, we are left unconfined by time. Night after night, we venture into realms of our past without the framework of time. Last night, we could have been four years old and confronting the giants and dragons of the unknown world. Last week, we could have been growing old and confronting the fearsomeness of death and dying. Another night, we could have visited with our mother who has been dead some 20 years. The boundaries of time are erased in our dreamwork, much as they are in those experiences remaining from horrific trauma left unintegrated in our sense of self. The trauma experience can now only be tolerated in this altered state of dream reality and in the split reality of the past and present (and then only in short, intense bursts).

The experience of receiving terrible news and being haunted by that experience for days afterward is no doubt rather common. This terrible news may then be forgotten for a moment, with a temporary sense of relief. Perhaps you awaken some morning feeling good, and then, in a rush of dread, the news revisits. The crushing reality is on you once again. This rather common experience gives some hint as to the reality of horrific trauma experiences revisiting the present.

THE STORY OF JULIA

Julia entered therapy many years ago in an attempt to deal with the pain of her depression, hopelessness, and inner sense of brokenness. She was vaguely fearful all the time. It remained very difficult over the years for her to focus on the depths of her pain. In place of comprehension, there was constant warfare with the present. Her rage and anger at events and people around her always seemed to be her way of compensating for the pain and hurt deep within her.

Julia experienced severe pain in her stomach, but medical workups could never confirm that anything was physically wrong with her. The occasional numbness in her limbs could not be understood either, but the symptoms were treated. Her pain and hurt seemed to be interminable. Her frantic searching for an explanation for her lingering inner pain continued year after year. The pain in her stomach came to be known as "the shotput in my gut." In her fear and rage, she saw dismembered arms flailing in front of her. Sometimes, she would beat her head with her fists or slam it against a wall. For relief, she would wrap herself in a large blanket and, in a huddled position on the bed, rock herself to sleep.

Julia is, however, a very functional woman. She is a professional in several fields and an excellent mother of three children. She contributes a great deal to her community through her involvement in many local activities. She has used therapy in a marvelous way over the years and has built for herself an excellent network of family and friends to help keep herself functioning and growing.

Recently, Julia underwent a period of severe stress as a result of a daughter's critical illness. Julia experienced her daughter's severe pain a year or so later in flashbacks of great intensity. In the flashbacks, Julia eventually became the victim instead of the daughter. In tapping into her daughter's extreme helplessness, she was soon able to tap into the core issue of her own helplessness in a profoundly new way. In the process of therapy, she reexperienced her own helplessness as an infant. Her mother had become mentally ill when Julia was about ten months of age. Throughout the course of therapy, it had been assumed that this must have been a critical period for her as a child. Now, however, she was able to reexperience the helplessness of her infant self. The flailing arms were her own, as she lay helpless and hurting in her crib; their random movement was the only stimulation known to her in that abandoned state. The "shotput in her gut" was now connected with the intense pain of her hunger, rage, and neglect that was unrelieved by her withdrawn and ill mother. Julia's only relief came from her farmer father, who came in from the fields on occasion, and from older brothers too young to care for her needs, except in their own childlike manner. The rocking and the hitting of her head were now at a deep affective level, connected with the pain of her early neglect and abandonment.

As her past grew in present intensity, and was redefined and claimed as her own in the present moment, Julia experienced significant relief. The pain and rage that had been ever present were now placed at the source and had new meaning. The pain and rage fit; they were now authentic. There was no longer any need to search the present for the meaning of her immediate pain and anger, only to be further enraged that it was not there. At last she could begin to find solace in the Now.

REEXPERIENCING

Julia's story reminds us that memory, as we usually conceptualize it, is not an adequate way to talk about the presence of the past in the present. The concept "memory" does not adequately explain the "reliving" of the past by trauma victims. "Reexperience" is perhaps the best verb to use in talking about the process that trauma victims experience. To reexperience is to confront the past traumatic experience with many or all of its original manifestations.

We can easily understand why a woman who had been raped in an elevator would break into a sweat whenever she had to use one. Her physical memory has been reenacted. This is not just an intellectual recall–the body remembers too. Every cell in our body has memory. This is becoming more and more clear to researchers. Ernest Rossi, in his books *The Psychobiology of Mind-Body Healing* and *Mind-Body Therapy*, has, along with many others, contributed much to our understanding of memory as a total-system process. In very simple terms, the process works like this: Our mind remembers, our brain remembers, our body remembers, and our spirit/soul remembers. When powerful memory is recalled, the gut remembers, the legs remember, the arms and fingers remember–our entire system remembers. Every cell of our body has a memory process; the memories of some cells may even be prone to drug addiction, for instance. This physical phenomenon raises many new and radical questions for our traditional understanding of memory, addiction, mental illness, emotional imbalance, and spiritual well-being.[2]

ROLFING

During the 1970s, my wife and I went through therapy known as "Rolfing," which derives its name from its originator, Dr. Ida Rolf.[3] Rolfing is a physical type of therapy based on the premise that the body is the repository of emotional memory: When a child is struck by someone, his or her body stores the pain and the response to the pain. The therapist, known as a "Rolfer," works with the fascia of the muscles to release them from chronic tension. It is a rather painful process that normally lasts for ten sessions of very deep muscle massage. When pain is released, however, there is often a powerful emotional connection of the pain to some past memory. When the therapist worked inside of my mouth, for example, I had a complete full-mouth Novocaine reaction: my entire mouth went numb for about two hours. Needless to say, I was soon in touch with the bitter memory of being held by my father while the old family dentist pulled my teeth. (I must have been eight or nine at the time.) It was not a memory that had been available to me without searching. It was, however, present in my mouth with just a bit of deep muscle probing.

My wife Jean, through the process of her own Rolfing, was put in touch with many pains of childbirth. When her muscles were rolfed, memory was physically released. Her realization of this came about because she remembered she had been teaching nursing on the OB floor of the hospital on Friday and had our first child on that same floor on Monday evening. She was, of course, the model patient, nurse, and instructor. Her own body remembered the pain in ways that her mind could not remember.

STATE-DEPENDENT LEARNING

Ernest Rossi and others are writing much these days on what is called "state-dependent learning." Basically what this means is that what a person learns in one state of being is remembered most vividly in that same state of being. This principle came to the fore some years ago in work with drug-addicted people. What had been learned in a drug-induced state was best remembered in that same drug-induced state. Many college students can verify this type of experience: studying all night under the influence of amphetamines does indeed enable one to retain significant material. Unfortunately, that material is not recalled the next day during the examination if the student is in a non-drug-induced state. The material is simply no longer available. However, the material will be recalled to a very high degree in a second drug-induced state using the same type of drug.

Understanding that we human beings are to a great degree a chemical and electrical system, we need to be in touch with this reality that what is learned in one physical state of being will be recalled in a similar state of being. To be placed in a totally helpless physical position or to be physically threatened causes us to reexperience past events that took place while we were in a totally helpless physical position or physically threatened. A Vietnam veteran's fear of being "locked up" is more than a fear of being placed in a mental hospital for treatment and losing his freedom of movement. His fear is the fear of reexperiencing a state of being physically helpless. If a Vietnam veteran who had been wounded in combat had to now be placed on a gurney and given sedation for an injury, he would most likely reexperience that wartime injury and its accompanying pain. This is much more than memory. It involves once again knowing the full impact of the original helplessness and experiencing psychic and physical pain of that past event once more.

RECREATING THE MOMENT

We actually know this already–we know how to help "recreate the moment" in order to recall the mood, atmosphere, feelings, and memories of the original moment. We know that words alone do not do it. Ritual, in its best form, does recreation for us. The water, the oil, the smell, the taste, the movement of the body all come together in ritual to set the power of the past into the context of Now. This is especially true for holidays: The last mangled ornament on the tree, the special dishes at Thanksgiving, and the eggs dyed at Easter all create stronger memories of the past than do words. When we add to these outward forms our own inner states of body, mind, and soul that connect with inner states of the past, we have a reexperience of great proportions.

Even as we strive to recapture the memories of holidays or romantic moments, we–with greater effort perhaps–do all we can to avoid the states that create for us pain and rage. Those physical, mental, and emotional states that recreate states of past trauma are avoided at great cost. This is one side of the truth. The other side is that often the previous state is recreated in order to attempt to alter that previous state. This is, no doubt, one of the main reasons why people find themselves over and over again in those crisis moments that cause great pain. They hope against hope that by reentering that previous painful state, things will be different. They come up with any number of rationalizations: "This time, she will learn to love me"; "This time, he will treat me with respect"; "This time, I will be able to help her see that I really do love her"; "This time, we will really connect and he won't walk out"; or "This time when I'm hurt, they will see my pain and love me."

We all want to be masters of our own destiny. We want to be in charge, in control, and making the decisions that shape and form our lives. Modern psychology is filled with theories about people's drive to act on their life's choices. The cognitive theories tell us that "we are as we think." There is, of course, much truth to this, but it is also true that much of who we are has been shaped by who we were; this is especially true for trauma victims. That unresolved self comes back to our present experience over and over again. More than we are often willing to acknowledge, the past invades our present and shapes the nature of the moment. We rebel against this invasion with a good deal of vehemence. We do not wish this past reality to be true. We spend much time, energy, money, and commitment to avoid the reality of who we have been. Still, as the saying goes, "You can take the boy out of the country, but you can't take the country out of the boy." That which we have been stays with us. It may have, for the most part, become unconscious, but it is nonetheless presently active in much of who we are.

FORGETTING

This present era is not a time when we easily acknowledge either the realities of our biological nature or the realities of our past (and especially those of our traumatic past). American culture is often characterized by a commitment to not remember. We have a tendency to fall into a public amnesia about many issues in our past. The Vietnam War era is a classic case in point. Veterans tried to forget, families tried to forget, our nation tried to forget. Perhaps confusion over the war's purpose was too great. Maybe we all needed time to integrate what was a traumatic national experience. The Vietnam War, Watergate, and President Nixon's resignation all represented events that did not correspond with what many Americans believed their country stood for. Our identity as a nation could not tolerate a Mylai, a military defeat, or a president who resigned in disgrace. There were no victory marches in the wake of the Vietnam War. There were no grand moments when the U.S. stepped forward and invited the enemy to surrender, as we did at the end of World War II. There was no grand commitment to peace and the cooperative rebuilding of a nation destroyed in war, as we had seen in Germany and Japan. Instead, there were a million people slipping out of Vietnam in fragile boats, committed to finding freedom or dying. We opened a few back doors to Vietnamese refugees, but, for the most part, there was never a total U.S. commitment to rebuilding war-torn Southeast Asia. We were too committed to forgetting. I suspect that the massive display of support for Desert Storm is related to the years of forgetting and

pain. At last, there was a moment to seize with some degree of hope-
fulness–and our wounded national psyche seized it. Desert Storm
happened quickly and called many in our country to "grab hold" and
attempt to undo history. Our country was strong and powerful once
again.

A parallel forgetting process was going on with individuals. The
men who had fled to Canada to avoid the draft returned home after
the U.S. government granted them amnesty. The veterans from Vietnam, men and women, melded into the quiet corners of our country
and tried to pretend it was over. I hear stories over and over again from
veterans who said they lied about serving in Vietnam. They lied
because the individual and public pain was too great to remember.
Even those who remained in the military often refused to wear their
official patches indicating combat service in Vietnam. Medals and
awards were often not worn on uniforms because the pain of rejection
and ridicule was too great.

During the Vietnam War, members of the military were required
to travel in uniform when using public transportation at military
expense. I had been at a retreat at a Roman Catholic monastery in
Silver Spring, Maryland, during the week of the violent confrontation
between National Guardsmen and students at Kent State University.
Like many others, I was very troubled by the deaths of the four
students. I was especially troubled because both my wife and I were
graduates of Kent State. I also knew the president of Kent State at that
time, Dr. White, as well as the Episcopal Chaplain who served with
the National Guard troops there. I made a very conscious decision not
to fly out of National Airport in Washington, D.C. in uniform that
next morning. To not be able to fly out of the nation's capital in
uniform presented a radical conflict. Symbolically, it was the end of
ends for me in many ways. As I remember it now, it was not long
thereafter that the military changed its regulations regarding wearing
a uniform while flying at military expense. The uniform would no
longer be required. Paradoxically, this change was accompanied by
shifts in the way the military conducted its business. The end of the
draft, the beginning of the volunteer Army, and the uniform regula-
tion change all indicated that the military was becoming more "professional" and less a civilian institution with professional leaders.

Young men and women in uniform soon disappeared from public view. The military identity was to be forgotten.

THE BEGINNING OF HEALING

The building of the Vietnam Memorial in Washington, D.C. in 1985 was a milestone for those who suppressed their pain for so long. Collective and individual memories of Vietnam and the Vietnam era burst forth in a blaze of awareness. Men and women came out of darkened dens and bedrooms, the woods, and obscurity to march in ragtag uniforms and be, in a small way, welcomed home and to take part in the healing that was so much needed. It was then that I began a series of Vietnam Veteran Support and Therapy Groups. This series grew out of my experiences at the Tuskegee Veterans Hospital, where I had recently been dealing with my own repressed and newly found evidences of trauma. After five years, many have gone through the group to find varying degrees of peace and meaning in their lives. It is within the context of meeting with fellow veterans that I have learned the most about PTSD. It is here that I have seen the flesh and blood of the disorder. My theoretical understanding comes from many other sources.

That tenth anniversary of the end of the Vietnam War and the building of the Vietnam Memorial broke open a floodgate of healing activities that convinced me over and over again that, as a nation, we have gone through the same stages the wounded individual does in experiencing trauma and healing. It is not a steady progression by any means. It is ragged in that healing takes place, followed by periods of regression, and then new healing follows. So it is in the life of the individual and nation.

At this point, I would like to share with you two composite stories of men who have come into the Vietnam Support and Therapy Group since 1985. Although I have talked with a number of women who served in Vietnam, and they have shared the pain of their recovery, none have been part of the ongoing support group. The group has been made up almost totally of men who served in combat, either in combat arms or in critical combat-support activities. Over the years, men from the Army, Navy, Marines, and Air Force have been part of the group–some of them veterans of both Korea and Vietnam. The group members have served as a microcosm of the war. Their common postwar experience represents a picture of the broad range of difficulties experienced by most Vietnam veterans following the war.

THE STORY OF BURT

Retired after 23 years in combat arms in the Army, Burt had spent five years in Vietnam. An alcohol problem made it easier for him to remain in Vietnam rather than deal with it stateside. He went numb, both emotionally and spiritually, early in his initial tour. He did not begin to revive until he was sober for about 60 days, five years after his retirement. In his present sobriety, he remembers with clarity the awfulness of Vietnam. He recalls the horror not only of the events but also that of his psychic numbing, which did not register until now. He sleeps with lights on and the television playing all night. His dog lies at his side, listening along with him. This is all a design to keep him from sinking into the past, where he would then be lost for hours. To stay vigilant, he conducts "guard duty" all night, two hours on and two off. The cycle is unbroken. The TV helps him stay in the present, which allows him to keep most of his conscious mind intact. That way, he can make it through the night and be ready for work the next morning. Without fail, he reports each Monday evening for group therapy. He listens with great interest as each man tells about his week. He wants to know the news of those missing. The group setting reinforces the fact that he will be missed and "reported on" if he misses. He belongs, and this makes all the difference in the world. Here, his nighttime rituals are understood, as are his public behaviors of always sitting with his back to the wall, or always sitting where he can face the entrance in a restaurant, or avoiding crowds and unruly situations. Here, he can laugh and be at ease.

THE STORY OF PETER

Peter never touched land in Vietnam. He comes to the group every Monday he can. He never smelled the jungle or tasted the fear of close combat. He served aboard ship along the coast of North Vietnam for two tours. He saw Vietnam–both North and South–from a great distance. What does he live with? What forces him back week after week into the comfort of the group? The fact that he is understood here. Others know and accept the reality of his horror and trauma. No one else has been able to do that. He has never been able to tell anyone else. As a young sailor, he went overboard time and time again to rescue downed pilots (or what remained of them). Into the Gulf of Tonkin he went, with a thin rope to pull him back when necessary. In he went with a thin rope that would be cut if the ship got into trouble and had to leave. In he went to perform his grisly task. Heads, arms, legs, and parts of torsos he pulled from the water were placed into plastic bags to be shipped home. He always went in hoping to pull a live pilot aboard. He never did–only parts of pilots. His buddies watched from aboard ship, with carbines ready to shoot the giant sea snakes that infested the waters. Each time he went in, Peter remembered the sailor who had been washed overboard in the Atlantic a year or so before. It was nighttime then, and they had searched for the sailor as best they could. However, they were unable to find him. The sailors along the rail could hear him shouting to them from the darkness of the night. That voice still keeps Peter awake often.

As the power of reexperiencing is more and more appreciated, the pain of the victim is seen as more present and much more relevant. This is good news. Having come to this point means that there is hope for understanding and treating the trauma victim. We have come to a broader appreciation of what the reexperiencing of pain means. We now see it as being in the present and beyond the ordinary understanding of memory. The next major hurdle is appreciating the reality of the cut-off part of the self. A victim of severe trauma is a person with a fractured ego. There is a part of the self that is no longer invited into the center of who we are.

THE EGO AND THE I

From Bruno Bettelheim's book *Freud and Man's Soul*,[4] we learn that English translators of Freud did him injustice when they translated his use of the German word *ich* (meaning "I") as "ego." They also mistranslated his use of the German word *es* (meaning "it") as "id," and his use of *superich* (meaning "oversized 'I'") as "superego." It would be much clearer for us to acknowledge the reality that our sense of "I" is incomplete, rather than that our sense of "ego" is incomplete. "I" belongs to me. "Ego" is an intellectual term found in textbooks. Horrific traumata shatter what "I" think of myself.

NOTES

1. Mason, Steve, *Jonny's Song: Poetry of a Vietnam Veteran* (New York: Bantam Books, 1986), p. 51.

2. The following books are recommended for a review of this subject:

Rossi, Ernest L. *Psychobiology of Mind-Body Healing* (New York: Norton, 1986).

Rossi, Ernest L. and David B. Cheek, *Mind-Body Therapy,* (New York: Norton, 1988).

Ornstein, Robert and David Sobel, *The Healing Brain,* (New York: Simon and Schuster, 1987).

Cousins, Norman, *Anatomy of an Illness,* (New York: Simon and Schuster, 1987).

Pelletier, Kenneth R., *Mind as Healer, Mind as Slayer* (New York: Delta Books, 1977).

3. Dr. Ida Rolf was the founder of Structural Integration, better known to the public as "Rolfing."

4. Bettelheim, Bruno, *Freud and Man's Soul* (New York: Delta Books, 1977).

Chapter 4

Post-Traumatic Stress Disorder–
A Spiritual Diagnosis

And then, when pressed with burdens and troubles
too complicated to put into words and too
mysterious to tell or understand,
how sweet it is to fall back into His
blessed arms, and just sob out
the sorrow that we cannot speak.

–Anonymous

This is a good place to shift our emphasis. We have up to now looked at the lives of a number of people who live and function with PTSD. We have looked at the profound impact this condition has on their lives at all levels. We have reviewed the material from the current American Psychiatric Association manual, DSM III-R, which defines PTSD in clinical terms. We have spent time with people struggling with brokenness and chaos in the midst of PTSD. In this chapter, we will begin to look at PTSD from a perspective that views it as a spiritual disorder as well as a mental, or functional, disorder.

Horrific traumata destroy spiritual well-being. The most corrosive impact of horrific emotional trauma is to be found in the spiritual fabric of persons. This is where the prolonged damage is created. This is the facet of the illness so often overlooked by the mental-health systems of our country. This is where medicine and the normally established practices of insight, behavior, and cognitive therapies have less efficacy. The condition of PTSD is spiritual at the deepest levels. This is where spiritual insight and community and relational-based approaches are most efficacious.

One of the pieces of good news in contemporary times is the growing reality that we have moved beyond the false distinctions created by early science. Descartes' bifurcation of mind and body and body and spirit no longer makes sense in our era. A human is a creature of mind, body, and spirit wonderfully made without division. After centuries of ripping humanity apart into segments of various ownership, we are more able to view ourselves as creatures created totally whole, as one being. There is a sense that we can once again appreciate the healing of the blind man at the pool of Siloam. This blind man, who had received mud and spit from Jesus as instruments of healing, reminds us of our own humanity, we who come from *humus*. There is a deliberateness about this healing on Jesus' part and on St. John's part. The neat intellectual distinctions of mind, body, and soul do not exist in this story. This is a blind man with a spiritual condition who is healed by Christ using spit and dirt. Medicine, psychology, theology, and physics enable us–at their best–to see ourselves as being in touch more with our wholeness than with our separate parts. Our views of illness, health, and our spiritual life are more in touch with the fact that body, mind, and soul are intricately interwoven into the wholeness of a person.

When we then speak of PTSD as basically a spiritual condition, we see it as having vast impact at the level of our spiritual understanding; yet it is no less important in terms of its physical impact on the physical nature of a person. PTSD creates havoc at all levels of who we are. Chronic fatigue, sleeplessness, gastric disturbances, and uncontrolled blood pressure are all exacerbated by the spiritual disturbances of PTSD. When we speak of the loss of hope, we are speaking of a diseased heart. When we speak of the loss of intimacy, we are speaking of chronic physical pain. When we speak of the loss of peacefulness, we are speaking of chronic hyperalertness. It is within this framework that we talk of PTSD as basically a spiritual dysfunction.

PTSD is a spiritual disorder not because the "person is not right with God" or that "God is not right with the person." It is a spiritual disorder because the person who experiences the full impact of PTSD has been impoverished by the loss of a series of vital spiritual attributes that are essential to living a full life. The following ten spiritual attributes are grossly affected when serious traumatic injury occurs.

SPRITUAL LOSSES

Loss of Hope

The hunter sat at the far edge of the deep pit into which he had fallen. He knew the pit to be at the end of a trail that was seldom used. He had struggled for the better part of the day attempting to get out. All effort had failed. He now sat thinking over his predicament. He smoked his last cigarette and felt his heart beating more quickly in his chest. The sky far above him looked like snow. Its gray overcast more than hinted of the first fall storm. Along with the promised snow, darkness was now moving into this part of the woods and the other end of the pit could not be seen. He was trapped. There would be no hunters along this trail again this fall. He lived alone, and he had told no one about his plans for today. Hope was eroding with each passing minute.

The hunter's predicament represents the loss of hope. Such a loss never occurs without reason. Hope is stripped away by events, facts, the collapse of ideals and promises, and the changing conditions around us. In assessing a person's spiritual condition, it is often important to make that distinction between helplessness and hopelessness. The hunter sits in the pit knowing he cannot get out by himself. He is helpless. He is dependent on others to get him out. He waits with hope for others to arrive. But his hopelessness is beyond his helplessness: Others have not only not arrived, they simply are not coming. The snow, the lateness of the season, and the fact that his plans were unknown to others all strip away the option of hope.

In making a spiritual assessment, it is important to have a grasp of the person's loss of hope. How profound is it? How systemic is it? How entrenched is it?

> All I want is to know Christ and to experience the power of his resurrection, to share in his sufferings and become like him in his death, in the hope that I myself will be raised from death to life. . . . I keep striving to win the prize for which Christ Jesus has already won me to himself. Of course . . . I really do not think that I have already won it; the one thing I do, however, is to forget what is behind me and do my best to reach what is ahead.

So I run straight toward the goal in order to win the prize, which is God's call through Christ Jesus to the life above. (Philippians 3:10ff, GNB)

It is clear to St. Paul and us that hope is a key to life. Without hope in living, there is no reason for being. To "forget what is behind me and do my best to reach what is ahead" may well be the goal for many; however, when that which is behind presents itself continually in the present–and with intensity and cruelty–then the process is shifted. When this process of hope is shut down and no longer functions, there is a severe spiritual crisis. It is this crisis of the loss of hope that calls our attention to the seriousness of PTSD.

Loss of Intimacy

When loved ones have been pushed away, when the caretakers have thrown up their hands, and when the last friends have slammed the door behind them, then trauma victims are free to contemplate the utter despair of their condition. It is then possible for them to finally touch the rage that has boiled deep inside, without fear of its erupting and causing serious injury to those around them. The victims of PTSD no doubt drive others away as an act of protection; victims know that only destruction and harm can be in the upcoming pathway. For this and other reasons, many Vietnam veterans have taken to the woods, the back bedroom, the workshop, or the darkness. To be alone, yes. But also to no longer fear the explosion of rage that could hurt those around them. Victims believe that the destruction that created their pain is so severe within them, that it will surely erupt and destroy those around them. As a form of prevention, victims often isolate themselves from their loved ones.

There is also the secret fear that the utter pain of the inner condition must be contagious. This secret fear is not unfounded, since the inner pain becomes systemic within the family and affects each member. The pain of the victim becomes the pain of each family member in its own way.

Pain is pain regardless of its source. The emotional pain of PTSD engrosses the victim to such a degree that there is neither energy nor reason to reach out beyond the self; the inner warfare is profound and consumes from within. The loss of intimacy does not mean the victim is uncaring, even though it is often perceived this way by those around him or her. At most, the loss of intimacy is related to the victim's inability to reach out beyond his or her all-consuming inner warfare.

Loss of Future

The loss of future is certainly connected with loss of hope, but perhaps they need to be kept separate for a better assessment of spiritual condition. Loss of future is perhaps more subtle than loss of hope. It is reflected in those bits of conversation that create an uncomfortable feeling in the listener: "Just pack me off to the nursing home when the kids are finished with me"; "There is no sense in retiring. There would certainly be nothing to do"; "No sense in having kids in this world"; "It's crazy to make plans. Somebody always messes them up"; "They never let you do what you want to do"; or "Life is just the same damn thing each damn day."

These are the words of people who have lost their future. The future has no meaning to them; it is nothing but the repetition of today, or worse. At some level, however, there must be the fear that to give tomorrow any power is to also give it the power to recreate the past. The future, therefore, must be envisioned as powerless, or at least as having less power than yesterday. The loss of future is the wish to make the world stand still, so it creates no further harm. It is the wish to be left alone.

Loss of Peacefulness

The victims of PTSD are in many ways the ghosts in our midst. Their search is the endless search for rest, for peace. They have a terrible conviction that there is no peace until the past has been undone. Their fearful search is for ways to undo the past and to recreate it with a proper ending. The nature of flashbacks is to bring the past into the present with the expectation that the ending will be different this time.

The inability to be at peace is expressed in a variety of ways: trouble sleeping, restlessness, and finding little enjoyment in the pleasure of the moment. The person who is unable to be at peace may seek to alter the present through drugs, alcohol, sex, and food. The inability to reflect, meditate, and restore are among the many ways of not being at peace. The loss of peacefulness can also be made more serious by the "busyness" that the local parish often encourages of its members. To generate endless activity is a sure way of avoiding the reality that caused the loss of peacefulness.

Loss of Healing Memory

The terrible reality of severe trauma is that it often eradicates the existence of positive, healing memories. We are all dependent on healing memories to encourage, inspire, comfort, delight, and heal us. Memories of having been loved. Memories of having been a success. Memories of sheer pleasure. Without these and other healing memories, we remain raw and broken. Very often, a victim's answer to the question "When were you last happy?" is "Never" or "I don't remember." The fact that life can be different from the brokenness and pain of the moment is not remembered and is, therefore, no longer an option. The task of healing, then, is in part recovering memories that are healing in nature.

Loss of Spontaneity

The inability to respond to the realities of the moment is the loss of spontaneity. To be controlled by predetermined past choices–regardless of the present events–is to live in an automatic manner, without the excitement of choice. To be unable to step outside to see an exceptional sunset because your shoes have to be polished is to have lost spontaneity. To be unable to be taken aback by beauty, to be unresponsive to a brief moment of joy, to be trapped and engaged in the mundane when joy is breaking out all around–these are some of the indicators that spontaneity has been lost and that a rigid veil of predetermined choices hangs over one's life.

Loss of Wholeness

The concept of the loss of wholeness is difficult to measure at first. Time is needed to fathom its destructiveness in the lives of people.

Basically, there is a loss of wholeness when only one or a few parts of one's personality become all there is. The pain, the injury, and the illness take on a life of their own, reducing the total person to the reality of the part. Nothing else exists or matters. The loss of wholeness is, however, quite a common affliction. Mothers become mothers and cease to be anything else. Men become workers and lose their life beyond the job. People become mental patients and lose their identity. People take on the nature of their illness and are no longer viewed as individuals with a history and a future. They become the "bipolar patient," the "heart condition" in Room 206, or the "difficult welfare mother" on the third floor.

Often, the loss of wholeness does not first come across as negative. The retained part is productive and positive. Those "lost" personality parts are not obvious unless a relationship is developed with the person; then the absence of other parts becomes clear. It is at this point that the pastoral relationship enables the pastor to view the person beyond what he or she presents in the public context of "coming to church" each week. To experience the loss of wholeness is to become only one of the parts of our being, and to lose all else.

Loss of Innocence

Learning that the world is destructive, that it can kill, and that it can rob a person of happiness is the erosion of innocence that begins in the midst of tragedy. Mothers do abandon children. Fathers do rape their daughters. Pastors do fleece the flock. Saints do become enraged. Nature does destroy. There is no place to hide. There is no going home again.

The loss of innocence becomes destructive when a victim's jaded view of life gives a cynical cast to all conversation and when it debunks the caretaker's efforts.

Loss of Trust

For a PTSD victim, the loss of trust can compound an already difficult situation. Having trust means letting go of a personal coping strategy that has not been working and trying something new. The decision to admit that "something's not working" is most frightening when you have had to rely on your own resources for years on end. To let that go and reach out for help is a serious act of trust. For a traumatized victim, it may require more courage than can be mustered at any given moment.

Loss of Awe

The last symptom of PTSD can be summed up as the inability to believe that there can be anything greater than that which inflicted the original pain. The power and majesty of God stands small in the face of the tragedy. The infinite has no meaning compared with the intensity of pain in that painful moment. All has been rendered insignificant by the awfulness of the trauma.

THE STORY OF BILL

Bill serves as a member of the vestry, and he finds the work very satisfying. Being on the vestry enables him to be involved with the church at varying degrees of intensity. In this capacity, he can be around the church on days when no one else is. He can come and go with a degree of freedom. Now perhaps this is strange to some, but for Bill it is necessary at times. He finds there are so few quiet places these days, so few places to be alone with little or no noise. And then again, there is the sense of holiness that churches and cemeteries generate for some persons. For Bill, vestry work is the best of both worlds. When the demands of his regular job pile up, he goes to the church and spends quiet time among the oak pews and flagstones. The bricks and mortar stand strong against the intrusions of the world; for a brief time, Bill feels safe and protected. On Monday, he will give vestry members a full report on housekeeping activities–including a detailed plan on preventive maintenance for the upcoming year–but for now, Bill is basking in the quiet of another world.

Bill sits in the back of the nave on the Epistle side. He sits with his back to the last pillar, the stone overhang hiding him from anyone coming into the church. In the blue haze coming from the stained-glass windows halfway up the nave, Bill has lost his focus. In that unfocused haze, his mind has projected the battles of his youth.

Bill's mother cried when she served him breakfast that morning 21 years ago. She served him breakfast with an attention to detail that she had not had for a long time. In fact, he could not remember it having been served quite like this before. His father stirred his coffee with slow, unconscious motions, the sugar having long dissolved. Bill's stomach was filled with anticipation and panic as he ate. He would rather have slipped out early that morning, but he knew this was the required ritual of saying good-bye to his parents. He was now in the car with his father. Bill looked at his mother's tears and also began crying. His father told him, "We'll watch out for your room and things, son; they'll be there when you get back." Not much else was said during the drive to the bus station. As Bill later watched from the bus window, his father seemed to walk away slowly. Bill thought perhaps his father was wiping tears from his eyes, but he could not be sure. He knew his own back smarted from the powerful hug his father had given him.

Bill lay in his bunk that night, and for many nights following, experiencing waves of pride and humiliation, fear and anger, hope and dread. He was never alone, except when he would awaken in the night for brief moments. Even then, he was surrounded by the night noises of the men around him and he was reminded that he was no longer an individual. He was connected to the man in front of him; the man behind him was connected to him; and so on down the long green line called the Army. Bill lay there and felt that connection. He breathed their air. He shared their darkness. He smelled their presence. And in it all, he felt his deepening sense of aloneness. In the pre-dawn hours, they were all up and moving into the cool air, another day having begun.

Bill moved from unit to unit, location to location. He learned new skills and new ways of dealing–all done while sharing that military connection to the man in front and to the man behind. Men were to his left and to his right. They changed names, but never positions.

The rank and foul air filled Bill's nose and lungs as he stepped off the plane in Vietnam. He stood on the hot asphalt, waiting to hear his name. He burned in the sun as his own sweat turned to mist and filled his nostrils. Other men stood to his left and right and to his front and rear; he felt alone and frightened in a strange and fearful world. The whispered word was passed throughout the ranks to look downfield.

They grew silent as they no longer listened for their names but simply watched as a lone airman on a forklift loaded aluminum caskets onto an Air Force cargo plane being readied for flight to the States. Before being pushed into the dark interior of the cargo bay, the caskets flashed a brilliant flood of sunlight off their metal surfaces. Even in death, there was a man to their front and rear and left and right, as they started the journey home.

Today was Bill's sixth day in Vietnam and his second day in his new and permanent unit. Today, he began his new assignment of burning human waste by pouring diesel fuel over it and stirring it with a metal rod until it was totally consumed. The smell would never leave his memory. Later in the morning, he received Communion. The pure white host was in sharp contrast to the dull-red clay dirt now becoming part of his hands and body. He received communion with a man to his right and a man to his left, with the priest to his front, and with men behind him waiting their turn. His mind flashed and locked on to the timeless image of men lining up before battle to receive the blessings of their gods. He felt he was but one man in a long line of men who never cease marching to altars and to war.

Bill saw the V-pattern of sweat on John's back in front of him. Watching it grow kept his mind off the horrid reality of the march through the jungle. He tasted fear today. No one had ever told him what it would taste like. Now he knew. It was one of those things you just suddenly know and never forget. Then the shots rang out. There was now a bloody hole in the sweaty V-pattern on John's back, and the blood stain grew darker as they waited for the medical choppers to come in. Another troop member, Smitty, had also been hit. His jaw was not fully closed, and his arm seemed to be trying to raise off the ground. The massive hole in his gut ended it all. When the choppers came, Bill helped place both his friends into the black body bags. The sound of the bag's zippers still echoes in his mind when he remembers his last glimpse of John and Smitty as the bags were drawn closed around them.

Bill's numbness came with the deaths of John and Smitty. The men to his left and right and front and rear became less familiar. While these strangers were zipped into their bags, he ate lunch. This may be the last break of the day. He did not even remember the casualties' names. He still feels the numbness.

The morning he returned from Vietnam, Bill's mother fixed him breakfast and his father asked him if everything in his room was the way he left it. Bill went out that night and got drunk. Then he went home with a woman he had met at the bar, had sex with her, and never even knew her name. He did the same thing almost every night for the next six months.

Today, Bill sits alone in the church. The blue and red haze filtering in from the stained-glass windows mingles with the lush green of the altar hangings. This strange mix of colors seems to highlight the ghosts of soldiers that march with him today, to his front, his rear, his left, and his right. During many Sunday Masses, Bill is reminded of his grim latrine detail in Vietnam: His nose is filled with the stench of burning human waste and the Communion host comes to rest in his clay-stained hands. He always moves back from the altar with deliberation, giving himself time to fast-forward 20 years in his mind. He then returns to his pew and family.

When Bill and his wife Susan were in marriage therapy, the therapist referred to Bill as stoic. He called him "unreasonably tough." Susan was not sure about this characterization of her husband. She knew him to be emotionally distant most of the time, but she was very aware that he had an emotional undercurrent that erupted with great force at odd times in their marriage. She had often thought this was due to Bill's having been raised as an only child in a home with parents who expressed little or no emotion. She was also aware that she purposely discouraged any show of emotion in their home in order to protect Bill. Susan was not sure when this had started or why she did it. It just seemed easier that way.

Some years ago when Bill and Susan had started marital therapy, it was following a point of sharp business growth for Bill. Their second son was three years old at the time and Susan felt she was losing Bill. She had said to the therapist, "Bill just is not emotionally present most of the time. We don't connect." Bill's reply was that Susan was too close and would not give him room to breathe.

Susan and Bill noted that they had met in college and had married just before graduation. When asked about losses, they both said that they had had no major losses in their lives. When asked about any separations in their marriage, they replied they had had none. Bill's combat experience in Vietnam was never mentioned as being relevant to the present situation. In the therapist's notes, Bill was described as "cold and fearful of intimacy."

A pastoral relationship with Bill would be difficult at best, since so much of his past would be alien to the parish's experience. Few parish members have, or would be willing to talk about, combat experience. Even parish members who did serve in Vietnam tend to not talk about it. In a typical parish situation, Bill's pastor may well have struggled with the whole issue of Vietnam in the late 1960s or early 1970s and found some resolution of his own by entering seminary. Men in the parish will represent a broad range of other experiences. The nation was split over Vietnam, and that division still remains in our national unconscious. Like Bill, the issue remains hidden, unresolved, not talked about. Perhaps those who marched for peace wonder in their own moments about that particular pathway toward justice and peace: the responsibilities of making a living have long since worn off the edges of many protesters' political commitment. Even the "burning spirit" that marked the Vietnam protests seems out of place in the usual run of things today.

THE STORY OF JAMES

James' stepfather held him up to ridicule over and over again. James saw the pain in his mother's eyes and wondered what it meant. Looking back on it now, he believes it was her divided loyalty that rendered her helpless. He cried himself to sleep many nights, wondering what it would be like to have a kind father. No one outside the family knew about the situation, and he found it impossible to tell his friends of his pain.

The day Mr. Jackson called James into his office and befriended him was a banner day in his life. He did not cry that night. Instead, he dreamed about what it would be like having an adult male friend at school. Two days each week, he worked around Mr. Jackson's office for an hour after school. Mr. Jackson told James about many interesting events and places. James felt very special, and he told his mother about his conversations with Mr. Jackson when he got home each evening. His grades improved, and he seemed to be dealing with his stepfather a little better now than he had.

And then came the betrayal. Mr. Jackson offered James a continuation of "this new and good relationship," but at a price. James would have to service him sexually on demand, or Mr. Jackson said he would see to it that James' life became even more miserable than it had been before. James was told to make his decision now: Either leave the office for good or come back to the supply room. James went to the supply room with Mr. Jackson, and he did so for the next eight months.

There is a plaque marking Mr. Jackson's service to the school and humanity hanging in the main hallway of the school. James sees it each time he goes to the school with his own nine-year-old son. James makes sure his own son is not dependent on others for fatherly attention. He hopes this makes a difference.

James finds it difficult to be close to older males. In his own reflective times, he finds that he still yearns for the approval of a father. Two partnerships later tell him that he keeps getting "taken in" by older men and is, in his own view, betrayed. He remains a loner. He finds it hard to be a team player. He feels cut out of the mainstream of male activity, and, in his own desperation, he feels asexual. To compensate for this, he finds himself being sexually demanding with his wife and, at the same time, cold and withdrawn.

James finds it hard to find comfort in his faith. He keeps getting caught up in betrayal: He wonders what it means to say, "Our Father . . ."

Chapter 5

Multiple Personality Disorder

Almighty God who settest the solitary in families
. . . .enkindle fervent charity among us all.

–Book of Common Prayer

THE STORY OF JANET

Janet sat at the kitchen table drinking coffee. The bitterness and temperature of the coffee helped keep her in touch with the present. She wanted very much to be present, to know what was going on. The kitchen was not too familiar. Dishes were in the sink–no doubt from her and her husband's breakfast. She stood up and walked into the den. Her coat and purse were in a chair. She opened her purse and found a bag from her drugstore. She opened it and found a bag of half-eaten candy and a new box of crayons. She went through her coat pockets and found two shiny stones, an acorn, and a few broken peanuts. She went down the hall toward her bedroom, holding one of the shiny stones in her left hand. It felt comfortable in her hand. She walked into the bedroom as though she had walked into the bedroom of strangers. There were objects and clothing she did not recognize. Looking around the room, she became aware that someone had made love in that bed last night; fear began to well up inside of her. The stones, the acorn, the crayons, and the forgotten lovemaking were coming together into a picture she did not want to remember. She quickly went to the shower and began to prepare for work, which took her mind off this morning's voids and fears.

As she sat at her desk at work, Janet breathed without difficulty for the first time that morning. Moving into her workday routine, she finally felt at ease. The events of the morning were now moved way back into her head and she was no longer aware of their pain. That night, as she prepared to go to bed, she saw a shiny stone on her dresser. She picked it up and dropped it into the trash without wondering, or remembering, how it got there.

Several weeks later, Janet awakened one morning in a motel room. She was alone, but obviously she had not been alone all night. She lay there quietly and, with great effort, attempted to remember events of the night before. None came. In time, she was able to remember leaving for work. It must have been yesterday. She became aware of her head. It hurt terribly. As she looked around the room, she noticed something that may have accounted for her headache: an empty bottle of bourbon on a dresser. She walked to the window and looked out. She recognized the street out front. She was not far from home. Within the hour, she took a cab back home. It was 8:30 a.m. With a rush, she was ready for work. The knowledge that her husband was out of town had surfaced as she had dressed in the bedroom. She arrived at work in good time, but returned home that evening both exhausted and numb. Her husband, Dan, arrived home on Friday evening and they spent a very ordinary weekend together.

As she walked into work on Monday morning, Janet found a note in her coat pocket that read: "Dear, dear Ann. How I love you. Always, Peter." She went into a panic and was on the phone instantly, making an 11 a.m. appointment with a psychotherapist who had been recommended to her some months ago by her minister. The note convinced her that she was insane. She did not want this confirmed, yet she did not want to live with her memory lapses any longer. Her life had become too fragile to continue as it had.

Early in therapy, Janet was both comforted and frightened. The therapist reassured her about her memory lapses: "Most of us experience lost time at some point in our lives." Somewhat more disturbing were such questions as: "What about the articles that appear out of nowhere–the crayons?" and "Have you always experienced periods of impulsivity?" She shared with the therapist the story of her childhood–normal, pleasant, loving parents, with no extraordinary trauma. As she continued in therapy, she felt less insane for the time being.

Dan and Janet stood together at the coffee hour following services at their church. A woman a bit older than Janet came up to her and asked how she had enjoyed the art show at the museum last Tuesday afternoon. Janet felt her whole being shrink as she nodded and said that the show had been wonderful. No memory registered for the art show, or for much of anything of last Tuesday. She moved away quickly from the woman and Dan, hoping to end this terrifying encounter. It was terrifying to Janet in the sense that she was a "nonperson" last Tuesday, at least in her own mind. She thought to herself on the way home from church that she must talk with her therapist about those "awful moments of nonbeing" as well as the "voices" that chattered in her head for days on end. She had assumed that these were the two confessions that would inevitably mark her "insane."

The next day in therapy, when Janet began quietly talking about the major loss of time periods in her life, her therapist asked her, "And who uses these time periods?" Without hesitation, she answered: "Judy, Beth, Ann, Kevin, and the others." These were the names belonging to the various voices she heard in her head day after day. She now sat in terror, believing that she had just admitted she was insane. Quietly, but with conviction, her therapist said, "Yes, I know Judy and Ann. They both have come to therapy at times during these last few months." Hearing these words, Jane was relieved. She no longer had to feel stigmatized by her self-imposed diagnosis of insanity.

Janet's anguish is at this point very private, except for her recent disclosure to a psychotherapist. Let us look at some of the pieces of her story thus far. In the first place, we have a young woman who has blocks of missing memory. These are periods of time that are, for her, totally blank; she may or may not have any missing feeling from the time. For example, she may feel physical pain or discomfort from the lost period of time and she may feel emotional pain as well. However, these are not just periods of time that are missing. The evidence around her indicates that she is very active during these periods of missing time and that she is often with other people. Peter and the woman at the art show are just two such people. These experiences are so familiar to Janet that she has, for a long period, not questioned their strangeness. She thought: Perhaps others experience this pattern of living; perhaps they just do not talk about it. This rationale had given her comfort often in the past, but now she is having difficulty maintaining that belief.

MULTIPLE PERSONALITY DISORDER

The events I have pieced together to represent Janet's struggle would most likely have pointed toward a very different diagnosis several years ago (namely, toward schizophrenia). Today, however, she would be diagnosed as having Multiple Personality Disorder (MPD), which is not a rare disorder. There is a rapidly growing field of treatments for the disorder, many of which have excellent results.[1]

By no means does everyone who experiences missing blocks of time have MPD. Many people with an alcoholic disorder have blackouts that account for lost periods of time and missed actions. Other conditions, such as a brain injury, can also account for missing blocks of time. The diagnosis of MPD depends on additional factors. While hearing "voices" is a classic symptom of psychosis, the manner and nature of the MPD patient's voices will be seen as clearly different from the psychotic patient's voices.

Another factor upon which a diagnosis of MPD rests is trauma that has been experienced over a rather long period of time (most often in childhood). This trauma was most likely inflicted by one or more people within the family structure. A most important aspect of MPD is that the person before us, Janet, will have no memory of the trauma. Thus, she talks about her ideal and perfect family in all honesty. The history of the long, ongoing trauma will only be known by one of the alter, or other, personalities. The alter personalities maintained by Janet–Ann, Beth, and Kevin–have been created at different times in her life and they represent a very elaborate defense system that has evolved over the years. Notice that one of Janet's alters is a male. It is normal for a person with MPD to have an opposite-gender alter personality.

UNDERSTANDING AND GRACE: THE PASTOR AND MULTIPLE PERSONALITY DISORDER

The parish pastor can play a most important role in the healing of the person with MPD. The pastor can help by bringing various aspects of parish life together in a healing matrix. This action is reminiscent of the Gospel healing where Jesus returned persons to their community for the continuation of healing. The first and foremost pastoral action must be enabling a person who you suspect has an MPD to enter good and competent treatment; the pastor should then arrange continuing support from the various parts of parish life. Dealing with MPD is much too complex to be undertaken by a busy parish pastor alone. My own experience indicates that during ongoing therapy for MPD, a person may need to be hospitalized on numerous occasions for short periods of stabilization. Any therapist who undertakes to work with MPD patients needs to have access to a psychiatric inpatient facility that is prepared to work with MPD patients. Without this medical support, the course of healing is often severely interrupted and, at times, could be life-threatening.

Once a good treatment process has begun, the parish pastor, in his or her ministry to the person with MPD, will need to understand the matter of "truth" for that person. For example, when Janet says she grew up in a loving and pleasant family, that is the "truth" for her. However, when you meet one of the alter personalities, you may well hear of a childhood of incredible abuse. This is also "truth." The present reality is that the "truth" is not shared with all the alter personalities but is reserved for the "keeper" of that reality. Thus, we can begin to see the elaborate defense system that has been established to enable Janet to live in the world of our reality.

The pastor also needs to understand the complete and complex shifting of alter personalities that can, and will, take place during an extended relationship with a person with MPD. More often than not, the choir member and the tramp will show up at different times during the pastor's relationship with this person. As pastor, you may find yourself looking at a person with whom you have had an ongoing pastoral relationship when, all of a sudden, the deep feeling begins to surface that you are seeing this person for the first time. The person looks like that person who has been in your study time after time, but, today, all has indeed changed. You have a gut feeling that something strange and unreal is going on; you are indeed right. You are sitting in the presence of an alter personality of someone who has lived a long time with MPD.

For the parish pastor, and for other people closely involved in the life of this person, the healing task is similar to the following circumstance. Suppose you were visited by a relative out of your past, an aunt you had not seen for 20 years. Suppose that she shared with you the fact that your father-her brother-had sexually molested her daughter over a ten-year-period. This abused cousin of yours had committed suicide last year. Can you imagine the crushing load of feelings that would descend on you at that time and for an extended period thereafter? This model of unearthed relationships is actually not even close to the crushing feelings felt by a person with MPD when she learns from her alter personality, via her therapist, that her father had indeed sexually molested her from age 6 to 16. The elaborate defense system of alter personalities had been created to avoid this knowledge. The pastor's role is to deal with the rage, hate, grace, and forgiveness that will intertwine in this person when the walls of unknowing have been torn down. This news of the trauma will soon be joined by the growing awareness of behavior engaged in by other alter personalities. Within these contexts, pastoral care will perhaps reach its highest point of grace.

I believe that it is necessary for us, especially as pastors, to stay in touch with our own lives in order to begin to know something of what reality is for the person with MPD. As we reflect, we grow more aware that remembering is a very subjective thing. The fact of remembering becomes the art of remembering, in which we reconstruct our own histories so that they are protective of our own painful past. Once we learn that the art of remembering tells us much about our pain, we are then ready to hear the histories of our clients and parishioners in a rather different way. We also begin to learn that our own egos and visions of self are so very fragile. The horrific is too damaging to the ego, the self, to be brought into the ordinary; so, it must be left where it is and where we cannot see it in the light of ordinary day. By the same token, the ordinary is too fragile to be brought into the horrific; so, the two spheres never meet if left alone. It is within the context of healing relationships that they meet and grow to the point of acceptance and healing. It is in this context that a redemptive parish community can be a true salvation for persons radically torn asunder by trauma.

There is another kind of selective remembering that reminds us that we have something in common with persons who have MPD: We can be in touch with events that we know happened-we were there-and yet we do not remember. We might think, "I remember going to the hospital. I remember going back to the house that night. I remember the funeral home. Yet I do not remember her dying. I know I was in the room when she died, but only because I have been told I was there." This is dissociation of the ordinary kind. This is a common experience that most of us will have sometime in the midst of everyday human living. Surely, it is out of this ordinary experience of avoiding our own pain that we are able to understand the serious dissociation of those who have suffered the ravages of incredible pain and who, as a result, have lost huge chunks of time and memory.

The pastoral message is that grace is operative within the confines of the horrific and of the ordinary. If we lose the sense that grace operates in both spheres, we have lost touch with a great deal of who we are as human beings, as pastors, and in so doing, we have lost touch with our understanding of God as a God of grace.

HEALING

For more than three years, Gloria Armstrong, a fellow pastoral counselor at the Pastoral Institute, and I have conducted an ongoing psychotherapy group for adult survivors of trauma. Over the years, 33 people have been a part of the group. Many have been referred to the group because a recent trauma (such as a rape, divorce, or a family death) had unlocked a longstanding trauma and its aftermath. Many were incest victims; others had suffered terrible physical and emotional abuse as children. At least five group members were experiencing severe ongoing dissociative disorders. Three were diagnosed with MPD. Almost all had attempted suicide, with several having nearly died. At least nine had been hospitalized in a psychiatric hospital at one time or another. The group is supported by the entire facility, which has a dual relationship with local parish churches and a private, non-profit psychiatric hospital. The Pastoral Institute is located on the same grounds as the hospital, and at times, group members have been hospitalized there and have continued in the group during their inpatient stay.

In the course of the group work, it became evident that all the group members had to hide from their past, just as they had had to hide from their childhood abusers. The group members' fear was twofold: they feared punishment for telling and they feared that no one would believe them if they did tell. In the painful process of victimization, hiding was the posture of safety. Their hope was that by staying hidden, they could remain out of harm's way. As victims, they hide in closets, under beds, at neighbors' homes. This physical hiding led to psychological hiding, from others and from self. Therefore, the first step in the healing process is *Becoming Known*.

The second step in the healing process is *Telling and Being Heard*. The old adage says, "There is healing in the telling of the tale." We need to understand that this part of the process is a two-way situation: There is both telling and being heard. To bare one's soul is not a once-and-for-all process. It is one that is begun and continued in an ongoing relationship. The telling-and-hearing cycle reinforces the process over and over again. Underlying the process is the need for someone to be believing. Often, we have to believe for each other until the other is ready to acknowledge and believe.

The third step in the healing process, *The Sharing of the Secrets*, takes place once the healing relationships have begun to form. In the case of multiple trauma victims, a long and painful process begins that will unfold over a very long period of time. It is during this coming-out period that the healing and holding relationships must be intact. Unfortunately, this is the most vulnerable period for both the therapist and minister, as well as for the client. My own clinical experience with those who have been further violated by their pastors or treaters in the treatment process has shown that sexual misconduct on the part of therapists and clergy has far too often created a whole new layer of trauma. The destructiveness of violating the healing relationship cannot be underestimated. At this point, the therapeutic helpers need to have constant supervision and professional support in order to remain objective and helpful. During the phase of sharing secrets, the pastoral and therapeutic task is to be "lovingly present," with grace and healing, both for the patient and pastor and/or therapist.

The fourth step of healing involves the process of *Validating of Self*. The trauma victims now grow into that wonderful awareness that they are more than they ever have believed. They are even more than the power that victimized them. It is in this phase that the victims can begin to confront the awful rage that is within them.

The fifth step is therefore called *Sharing of the Rage*. It is only in the sure knowledge of grace that the victims can confront the reality that, within their rage, they are as powerful as the horrific trauma that victimized them. In sharing this sense of rage, the victims acknowledge that their rage places them alongside those who made them victims. The power of the group, the parish, and grace enables the victims to come to know that they need no longer act on this rage for relief.

The sixth step is the *Hope of Restoration*. Victimization means brokenness; healing means restoration to self, others, and community. The parish, the psychotherapy group, or any other vehicle of healing becomes the crucible of hope for restoration.

The seventh, and final, step is *Going Beyond the Group*. So very often after being healed by Jesus, the healed person wanted to stay with Jesus; but Jesus would send them home. This is the task of every healing process. Healing takes place so that persons may leave that process and claim their rightful place within society.

NOTE

1. Two excellent books in the field are:
   Braun, Bennett G., Ed. *Treatment of Multiple Personality Disorder* (Washington, D.C.: American Psychiatric Press, 1986).
   Kluft, Richard P., Ed. *Childhood Antecedents of Multiple Personality* (Washington, D.C.: American Psychiatric Press, 1985).

Chapter 6

The Victim and the Family

Blest are they whose days have not
tasted of evil. For when a house
hath once been shaken from heaven,
there the curse fails nevermore,
passing from life to life of the race; . . .
I see that from olden times the
sorrows in the house of the
Labdacidae are heaped upon the
sorrows of the dead; and generation
is not freed by generation but
some god strikes them down, and the
race hath no deliverance.

–Sophocles, *Oedipus Rex*[1]

All that we have considered as destructive to the individual
through horrific traumata is equally destructive to the individual's
family. Whether the trauma is incest or war, there is some of the same
impact on the family. When individual family members are traumatized, ramifications are felt in the entire family. At times, of course,
whole families are traumatized, as in natural disasters or war. (The
Center for the Study of the Holocaust has even traced the transmis-
sion of trauma down generational lines.) We in the 1990s are all
inheritors of the severe traumata of this century: World Wars I and II;
the Great Depression of the 1930s; the Holocaust; the Korean War;
the Vietnam War; the Cold War; the mass disruption of millions of
refugees; the mass destruction of the Cambodian population during
the 1970s are just some of the many examples. I could go on and on.

As I write this, relief efforts are continuing to deal with the quarter
million people left homeless in the wake of Hurricane Andrew. All

this occurs in the same time frame with starvation in Somalia and bloodshed in former Yugoslavia.

On Thanksgiving Day in 1990, our son Andrew was called to active duty along with his National Guard unit, the 48th Infantry Brigade of the Georgia National Guard. They left for training in the Mojave Desert of California. As a family, we said good-bye to him shortly before noon on Christmas Day. It was a very difficult time for our family as it was for so many families. The holiday feeling of Christmas was tempered by Andrew's leaving and the inevitability of war in the Middle East.

MARK'S DREAM

Sometime after Andrew left for California, and we were anticipating his going on to the Persian Gulf, our youngest son, Mark, had the following dream. Not only does Mark have excellent recall of his dreams, he has willingly shared this dream for inclusion in this chapter on the family and trauma. I am including the entire dream to give some understanding of how deeply, on the unconscious level, members of a family share the view of trauma anticipated, and trauma experienced.

This is what I remember from my dream on Wednesday night. I walk into a church–it appears to be St. Thomas, or very similar. There is an eerie feeling about. I know I am at my brother Andrew's funeral. I go to the first pew on the left-hand side and take a seat next to one of my siblings. I look up at the casket and see Andrew lying there with a black suit on and his Army haircut. He is dead. I didn't know it was going to be an open casket funeral until I saw it. I feel a frightened sense of evil and grief. The sibling sitting to my right feels like Stephen or Andrew. Out of the corner of my eye, I see that it is Andrew, only he is dressed in a blue blazer; his hair is the length that it was before he went into the Army and he is thinner.

The next thing that I remember is that the ceremony has become decentralized and there are some kids playing with my brother's body. They have messed up his clothing and have opened his eyes. His casket is now pointing toward the altar and slightly to the right-hand side of the church. I notice that another body is on top of Andrew. I think to myself that this is very disrespectful and how dare they do that to my brother. Several more caskets appear and it's as if it's a multi-person funeral. Although in the dream this apparently isn't unusual, I nevertheless feel very sad and I feel like the sacredness has been thrown out. I feel almost violated.

My sister Sara and I are walking around the casket, toward the sacristy. As we walk, we look over at Andrew in the casket. The casket has become almost like a hospital bed, and it is tilted upward and facing us. Andrew is in a white sheet and his eyes are still open, though he is very dead. His eyes are a dark bluish-black; they appear to be made of glass or steel, and they follow Sara and me as we walk past. She seems to make a verbal note of how weird that is. I know that what's controlling the eyes is not my brother but something very sinister. Although I don't really see Sara, I know that she is the Sara from a few years ago, probably about the time that Andrew went in the Army. Someone tells us that there is a sort of shopping center where we can buy things to lay by the dead to pay our respects. It is a long mall-type hallway located where the sacristy is in reality. I see some poinsettias near the entrance, and I think Sara stops to look at them. I find myself further down the hall, holding a shovel. It's a fold- up spade with dried mud on it, like the one Andrew and Steve had in Boy Scouts. I get this for Andrew because I remember something that he said about how having a shovel and being able to dig somewhere was very important to him. (I really wish I could remember the exact wording of it, because I feel it was very profound in my dream.) I get the shovel; I have a feeling of sadness, but I also feel that in doing this, I have done something important for Andrew.

When I return to the church, I see some members of my family sitting in a pew, laughing and talking and (I think) drinking. I begin to be upset about it, but they are not paying much attention to what is going on in the church.

I look up toward the caskets and they are now shaped like crosses. They are tilted upward, but not quite standing. Andrew's is in the middle, with two other cross-shaped caskets on either side. The one to the far left is blurry, so my attention is focused on the one to the right. In it is an older man. I think there are children playing on this casket. The dead man in it seems disturbed, but is not quite able to do anything about it.

Somewhere in the midst of this, my brother Tom and I decide we have to go and straighten up Andrew's casket and his clothing and remove the other body from on top of him. No one else seems to care, but we feel it is very important. The coffin changes to a sort of ambulance-type structure, with Andrew on top of it. We are outside now, but we are also in the church. Thomas looks much younger than he is in real life, probably around his fifth-grade year.

I remember that Andrew died of wounds inflicted either in war or in training, so I decide to see what they look like. As I look on top of the ambulance, I see Andrew in the sheet again, with many scars on him. His foot, which is up near his side, is facing me. It is about a foot-and-a-half long with three sharp pointy-toe-like things. It seems to be made of very rough-hewn white plastic. It has a couple of holes (which look like they may have been done with a drill) on the bottom of it, and there are also a few slash marks on it. I step down and see Thomas trying to climb on top through a door in the roof of the structure. He is having some difficulty. I encourage him to keep trying, but he slips. I see he has been wearing some sort of breathing apparatus that is made of a hose that runs from a water pack to his nose. It has become detached and he is crouched on the floor, looking up at me desperately, as if he's struggling to try and fix it but he can't. This part fades away.

It is late dusk. I'm with my family on a sort of deck on the ocean. A friend of mine is here, and my brother-in-law Sam is here. We are all grieving and there is a vague sense of consolation about. I wander around this deck, saying to myself "I know I'm dreaming and I must find something to prove it." I kept looking. I think I finally accepted that it was no dream.

My task is not to analyze Mark's dream. I was, however, struck by how readily Mark was able to share the depth of his pain. In this one expression, we see the profound depth of our inner and unconscious connectedness.

TRAUMA AND THE FAMILY

Beginning with an in-depth study of Holocaust victims, researchers have increased their understanding of marriage and the family in the face of tragedy and trauma. In some sense, it would be almost impossible for us to find many families who have avoided the pain of severe trauma (especially in this day and age). My own family's experience, I am sure, is far from unique in sharing three generations of war from 1916-1990. My Uncle Luther served in France in World War I; three of my brothers served in World War II; two brothers served during the Korean War era; I spent my tours in Vietnam; and my son just returned from being activated during the Persian Gulf crisis.

A different kind of warfare continues on city block after city block throughout our country. The scope of horrific traumata on national and global scales is repeated time and time again in micro-events within communities and families. Added to this are domestic violence, sexual assault, drug-related crimes, and crimes against people. We live in an era when the experience of each and every family is partly framed by violence and trauma. There is no longer any doubt that "The sins of the fathers have set the children's teeth on edge." There is no doubt that the effects of trauma are transmitted though the generations.

In coming to some understanding of how to deal with the massive onslaught of trauma, I would like to turn now to the family. At the end of the marvelous movie *Moonstruck*, the family whose human frailties have been exposed throughout the movie stands around the table and drinks a toast "to the family." I have seen the movie three times; each time, I am thrilled when–out of the seeming chaos and destruction–there comes that grand salute to the family.

WHAT IS A HEALTHY FAMILY?

There is a rigorous battle going on within Church communities. To put it very simply, it is a battle between those who would define the family as that "ordained by God in the Bible" and those who would

press us to "know how to adapt" to the light of God's leading at the
end of this century. There are no doubt many markers on this battle-
ground, but I see Pat Robertson (and his Family Channel) standing at
one end and Bishop John Spong (Episcopal Bishop of New Jersey)
standing at the other. Both ask the question "What is the nature of the
healthy family in this last decade of the century?" By asking this
question, perhaps in this way, families may begin to look at their own
structures to assess their own level of "health" as a family.[2]

At a 1990 conference in Washington, D.C., 12 leaders in family
research met to talk about the characteristics of the "healthy family."[3] Nine characteristics emerged in a consensus of the basic dimen-
sions of a strong, healthy family. It should be remembered that this
list is only a beginning. It is neither conclusive nor exhaustive. Research on the healthy family is ongoing, and the structure of a healthy
family continues to be defined. I do think that the list is a good
beginning. I have chosen these nine characteristics as a way to orga-
nize my discussion about the nature of the healthy family.

1. *Adaptive Ability* refers to the family's ability to adapt to predict-
able life-cycle changes as well as to various levels of stress. In the
years between 1930 and 1990, the family has undergone enormous
change. During these 60 years, incredible stress has been placed on
the family, which has been forced to respond, to adapt, and to change.
Parental roles have changed, and education, for example, has radically changed the economic structure of the family. Today, few 16-year-
old sons contribute significantly to the support of the family, as was
so often the case in the 1930s. Today, young women often delay
childbirth until their thirties, in order to establish their careers. Regardless of these radical changes, many of which have been exciting
and creative, the family has still been able to be a place of care and
support. For instance, my family enabled me to receive a college
education. My brother Donald, his wife, Margaret, and their children
opened their home to me and enabled me to complete college. My
own children have been given the option to live at home and attend
a senior unit of the university system of Georgia, Columbus College.
At a time in their lives when personal responsibility and indepen-
dence are so very important to my children, this arrangement has
placed significant strain on our family to change and adapt. It has not
been easy, but it has often been creative.

2. *Commitment to Family* involves both the recognition of individual worth and acceptance of the value of the family as a unit. Some years ago, in the process of having children live at home well beyond what had been the norm during the past several decades, certain house rules were written in our family. I would like to share them, because I think they reflect the struggle to commit both to the family as a unit and to individual values. As our children graduated from high school, we offered to each of them this covenant: "You may live at home free of charge if you are enrolled in college. College and all expenses will be yours to meet, and you must keep the house rules." House rules were designed to enable each person to move from a more dependent status to a more independent status. Some of the major structured rules included:

- Communication about schedules will be clear and consistent.
- The house will know your whereabouts.
- Mutual respect for the life of each family member will be maintained. The person with the greatest need will have priority.
- The needs of the family take priority over the needs of individuals.
- Issues will be worked through with the person involved. If this cannot be done, the problem becomes a family issue. If the above fails, the parents remain the final authority.
- Destructive behavior will not be permitted within the family. Treatment, or a similar form of dealing with the behavior, will be expected.
- Contribution to the common good will be expected and maintained in the form of household chores, regardless of other commitments.

3. *Communication* refers to clear, open, and frequent communication patterns. It is one of the characteristics of healthy families that is most often cited.

4. *Encouragement of Individuals* refers to the family's ability to encourage a sense of belonging at the same time that individual development is encouraged.

5. *Expressions of Appreciation* involve consistently doing things that are positive for the other members of the family. There is a sense of delight in the family members and in the related feelings they share.

6. *Religious/Spiritual Orientation* is an area that the conference considered as important, yet there was no consensus about the particular aspects of religion that specifically characterize healthy families. The faith community needs to clarify and make this aspect known.

7. *Social Connectedness* refers to the family's connection with the larger society, extended family, friends, and neighbors. It also includes the family's participation in community activities, which often provide external resources to assist a family in adapting to change and growth and to coping with problems and difficulties.

8. *Clear Roles* means that there is a clear and flexible role structure in which family members know their roles and responsibilities. Thus, they are able to function effectively in both normal and crisis situations.

9. *Shared Time* refers to (1) family members sharing both quality and quantity time and (2) the degree to which the sharing is enjoyable for them.

If the "healthy" family has this set of characteristics, then it follows that the unhealthy family does not have them–or does not have enough of them. A question yet to be answered is, To what extent can a healthy family have only some of these characteristics? Certainly, a family may be healthy and yet have several areas that need work. What is clear is that the healthy family that has undergone traumatic stress as a unit will be severely tried in many, or all, of the areas discussed. Some family members may be more affected by the trauma than others, and their resulting disabilities will have their own effect on everyone else. It is equally clear that the family–healthy or not–that includes one or more members who have undergone some type of traumatic stress will find its ability to remain, or to become, healthy severely challenged.

Charles Figley, editor of the *Journal of Traumatic Stress*, has been the leading writer on treatment of families whose traumatic stress has become part of their structure.[4] He notes five key phases in treating stress disorders.

Figley's first phase involves "Building Commitment to the Therapeutic Objectives." He writes that "commitment and trust are critical elements in psychotherapy treatment methods. The early phase of intervention is primarily dedicated to this end."

In the second phase, "Framing the Problem," Figley writes that family members "disclose how they view the problem." During this phase, family members will be allowed "to articulate their own understanding and acceptance of these realities among all family members" and also "help the family list wanted as well as unwanted consequences of the traumatic event." In addition, the family will need to "encourage disclosure about the purpose and utility of the current psychotherapy, and, in the process, . . . promote new rules which permit and encourage self-disclosure among all members during session." By doing so, family members will "shift attention away from the 'Victim' and toward the family system that has been victimized."

According to Figley, the third phase "Reframing the Problem," is "the most critical. Here the therapist must help the family generate and assemble the various feelings and perceptions associated with the traumatic event. Eventually, the therapist must help the family develop a healing theory about the event and possible future events."

In the fourth phase, "Developing a Healing Theory," Figley believes it is "critical that the therapist allow the family to develop a single, unifying healing theory . . . [by] reframing statements to fit a pervasive family healing theory."

In the fifth phase, "Closure and Preparedness," the "final session should convey a sense of accomplishment: that the family did it mostly on their own; that the therapist only served as a helper. They should be encouraged to write or call the therapist at any time, but urged to use the skills and insights they have developed in session to try to handle their own problems as they emerge."

NOTES

1. *Oedipus Rex,* from *The Oedipus Plays of Sophocles,* translated by Paul Roche, translation © 1958, renewed © by Paul Roche. Used by permission of New American Library, a division of Penguin Books USA Inc.

2. Napier, Augustus Y. and Carl A. Whitaker. *The Family Crucible* (New York: Harper & Row, 1988).

3. "Healthy Families Featured in Washington Conference," *Family Therapy News,* July/August 1990, p. 8.

4. Figley, Charles. "A Five-Phase Treatment of Post-Traumatic Stress Disorder in Families," *Journal of Traumatic Stress,* Vol. 1 (1988), pp. 132ff.

Chapter 7

Pastoral Counseling
and the Treatment Process

Christians affirm that counselor
and counselee must face a third unseen Person.
The Spirit of God operates in moments of
extremity and perplexity. Those who confess their
limitations and daily wait upon God
will find light rising up in the midst of darkness.

–Samuel Southard[1]

THE FAMILY OF HUMANKIND

The following remark has been attributed to many, but perhaps most often to Winston Churchill: "We design buildings and move into them and are defined by them thereafter." Not unlike buildings, theology defines much of who we are and how we function. Within the family of humankind, theology is being formulated. The formulation grows out of this very concept of the "family of humankind," for it is within the context of the family that the world's great religions are talking together in very different ways than in the past. This "fragile earth," our "island home" as the Episcopal Book of Common Prayer calls it, is no longer able to tolerate the enmity of the past; this enmity can no longer be seen as just, but must now be seen as sheer destruction. The *odium theologicum*, that proverbial hatred between contending theologians, is certainly not tolerable in a time when we are growing daily in our conviction that the family of humankind either stands together or dies together.

Several significant events during this century have called us to task. With the two World Wars, the Korean and Vietnam Wars, and almost continuous civil and regional wars, more humans have been killed in this century than have lived in all the previous centuries. This fact, coupled with increasing nuclear capabilities and nuclear stock-piling, must soon convince us that earth is indeed a fragile island home.

The "trashing" of our earth has become an increasingly popular metaphor. Perhaps the events of this century have created a condition not unlike PTSD within the psyche of humanity. A good case can be made for this in the context of Western society, with its quests for material wealth and numbness. These two pursuits are not unlike one another: both work well in helping us to forget the awfulness that is just beyond our seeing. And what is left in the wake of such pursuits? The trashed humanity of the poor and homeless. The trashed human-ity of the mentally ill. The trashed humanity of the aborted. The trashed humanity of the elderly. No wonder we in the West awaken at night in cold sweats and a common fear of being too close. No wonder PTSD is a growing phenomenon in our time. It is our com-mon illness.

Both Marshall McLuhan's concept of the "global village" and our growing concept of the "family of humanity" were clearly evident in the breathtaking world events of late fall and early winter 1989-90-the dramatic changes in Eastern Europe and the apparent disintegration of the Soviet Union. President Havel of Czechoslova-kia, in an address to the U.S. Congress in February 1990, spoke of the need for politics to grapple with serious moral issues. This is a new spark in the body politic of this century. It dovetails well with the growing body of theological thought that attempts to speak to the growing human and ecological hurt of our era.

As the world's great religions cautiously look toward each other, there is a growing commitment to embrace each other's sense of power, mystery, and commitment to a common humanity. Within this cautious embrace, there is a marvelous and freeing understanding that God is even greater than we had hoped while we were locked in our own isolation. From within the context of Christianity, there is a growing realization that the Incarnational truth is even more perva-sive than we dared hope. As St. Paul preached a sermon about the "unknown god," so do we find this god confirming what we have grown to know within the context of our Incarnational awareness. When Thomas Merton spent time with his brother monks of the Eastern traditions, he hoped to confirm this growing and powerful awareness.

Many years ago, in the midst of the monsoon season in northern South Vietnam, a group of Buddhist monks arrived at the Army compound where I served as chaplain. They had gathered about one hundred burlap bags of french bread for villagers who were cut off from food sources because of the heavy rains. They asked if we could match their resources with our helicopters and fly them and their bread to the hungry villagers. I will never lose sight of that sacramental mission in the pouring rain. Buddhist monks, an Episcopal priest, and Army gunships joined together to bring bread to the hungry. To me, that moment represented what religion is all about. The immediate crisis and our theologies formulated the response.

GOD WITH US

Within the family of humanity, the sharing of theological intimacy is a new and difficult process. Long-held suspicions and hatred as well as past hurts and pain have blocked the free flow of understanding and awareness. But these are coming around slowly now. As this growing understanding takes place, the realization that *God is* is claimed for all who are part of the family of faith. The next step, the realization that *God is with us*, is likewise claimed and shared. And finally, there is the realization that God and humanity are *at one* on some mysterious level.

This three-tiered awareness of our common conviction comes not out of theological textbooks but out of the sharing of humanity's common pain. An industrial gas leak that kills thousands in India. Hurricane Hugo in South Carolina. A devastating earthquake in Iran. All of these events were televised worldwide just minutes after they happened, providing a common bond of humanity. The revolution that took place in Eastern Europe between 1988 and 1990 and the failed coup in the Soviet Union in the summer of 1991 bound the rest of the world by the intimacy that television can provide. However, it is a very fragile and fickle intimacy, which can be replaced instantly by the next momentous event. Still, television is a means for global intimacy nonetheless.

What we say about God in our theology for dealing with our family of humanity and its manifest pains and struggles is at best a view based on our common images of God. These images evoke meaning from each of us from within the context of our own lives and experiences. This theology has a broad range of expressions, but none more clear than that presented by the Psalmist when he tells of God's wonderful knowledge of who we are:

> Lord, you have examined me and you know me. You know everything I do; from far away you understand all my thoughts. You see me, whether I am working or resting; you know all my actions. Even before I speak, you already know what I will say. You are all around me on every side; you protect me with your power. Your knowledge of me is too deep; it is beyond my understanding. Where could I go to escape from you? Where could I get away from your presence? If I went up to heaven, you would be there. If I flew away beyond the east or lived in the farthest place in the west, you would be there to lead me, you would be there to help me. I could ask the darkness to hide me or the light around me to turn into night, but even darkness is not dark for you, and the night is as bright as the day. Darkness and light are the same to you. You created every part of me; you put me together in my mother's womb. I praise you because you are to be feared; all you do is strange and wonderful. I know it with all my heart. When my bones were being formed, carefully put together in my mother's womb, when I was growing there in secret, you knew that I was there-you saw me before I was born. The days allotted to me had all been recorded in your book, before any of them ever began. (Psalm 139:1-16, GNB)

This intimate view of God's knowledge of us and of His absolute presence with us serves well as a cornerstone for a theology of God with us in the midst of pain and hurt.

God is not humanity; humanity is not God. God and humanity are inseparable. God is unknowable apart from knowing humanity. To speak of God is to speak of humanity; to speak of humanity is to speak of God. Emmanuel, God with us.

> I was hungry and you fed me, thirsty and you gave me a drink; I was a stranger and you received me in your home, naked and you clothed me; I was sick and you took care of me. . . . When, Lord, did we ever see you hungry and feed you, or thirsty and give you a drink? When did we ever see you sick or in prison, and visit you? The King will reply, I tell you, whenever you did this for one of the least important of these relatives of mine, you did it for me! (Matthew 25:35-40, GNB)

When God called Sarah and Abraham, he cast his lot with humanity. When he led the former slaves from Egypt, he joined with humanity. When he entered Bethlehem as Mary's child, he made that connection with humanity absolute. When God cast his lot with humanity, the Word became flesh and dwelt among us. Christianity has flipped this around too often by saying, "Seek God out there," when God has made it clear that "The Word became a human being and full of grace and truth, lived among us. . . . The Word was in the world, and though God made the world through him, yet the world did not recognize him. He came to his own country, but his own people did not receive him." (John 1:10-11 and 14, GNB).

"He came to his own country, but his own people did not receive him." How we want to make that God-in-Christ a stranger, not one of us. The tendency is always to reject his at-oneness with us. The theology for survival at both an individual and family-of-humanity level is to acknowledge this at-oneness with God.

PRAYER

In St. Luke's Gospel, Jesus' disciples are unable to drive out a demon from an ill boy. When they privately asked Jesus why they could not do this, he replied: "Only prayer can drive this kind out . . . nothing else can" (Luke 9:29, GNB).

While working within the context of human emotional trauma, prayer has been very difficult for me. This difficulty comes from our history of prayer as asking. "Pray for me" has normally been heard, and said, as a request for me to be the person's advocate with God, to get God to change His mind. In this context, I quit praying a long time ago. Such prayer, for me, did not provide communication with the God among us. Many times, I have felt the questions no longer made sense (let alone the answers). Prayer, as I was hearing about it, did not seem to fit within this context. God was either so close to the tragedy of the hour that He certainly knew what needed to happen or else He had withdrawn so very far away that even prayer could not invite Him to return.

It was when I learned that prayer is simply stating the obvious that prayer once again became meaningful for me. I relearned the principle that prayer is most often not verbal. Prayer is often action. Work is prayer. Service is prayer. Being at peace is prayer. Being with another is prayer. To know this, and to claim this, places our life and energy into prayer. To be at prayer is to know that the person I am with is the Word made flesh. Not just once upon a time, a long, long time ago, but in *this* moment and in *this* person and at *this* time.

Prayer radically changes how life is seen and known. Prayer changes time. In prayer, there is no past and no future. Prayer is *being* with God or another person. In that context, there is only now. As fifteenth-century prelate and philosopher Nicholas of Cusa said:

> All time is comprised in the present or "now." The past was present, the future shall be present, so that time is only a methodical arrangement of the present. The past and the future, in consequence, are the development of the present; the present comprises all present times, and present times are a regular and orderly development of it; only the present is to be found in them. The present, therefore, in which all times are included, is one: it is unity itself.

The mystery of prayer is that mystery now becomes commonplace. That pain of the moment is at one with Jesus' pain on the Cross, and both are joined together at the Heavenly Banquet. The isolation of time no longer exists. Completion is always present within the context of being formulated, of healing within brokenness, of intimacy within isolation, and of peacefulness within chaos.

So we must understand that what we call the present moment is not now, for the present moment is on the horizontal line of time, and now is vertical to this and incommensurable with it. So Barth [Karl Barth] points out that the true, living life of man does not lie in historical time, nor is faith something that begins at a certain point in time and grows along time. He is really talking about another level of consciousness-another dimension. It is the Moment that "qualifies and transforms time," and all else, all that is taken as faith, belongs to the "unqualified time" of sleep. . . . If we could awaken, if we could ascend in the scale of reality concealed within us, we would understand the meaning of the "future" world. *Our future world is our own growth in now, not in the tomorrow of passing-time.*[2]

HEALING IN THE GOSPELS

When we spend time with the healing stories of the Gospels, we are struck by many things. One that stays with me is the fact that healing is always contextual. The meaning is always much greater than the healing: it reveals the power of God; it restores people to community; or it restores a person to family. In the cosmology of the New Testament, many of the healings have to do with demons. In our present cosmology, healings have much to do with the misuse of our own humanity: not valuing our humanity; denying its full potential; or giving in to destruction and misdirection.

When Jesus came to the territory of Gadara on the other side of the lake, he was met by two men who came out of the burial caves there. These men had demons in them and were so fierce that no one dared travel on that road. At once they screamed, "What do you want with us, you son of God? Have you come to punish us before the right time?"

Not far away there was a large herd of pigs feeding. So the demons begged Jesus, "If you are going to drive us out, send us into that herd of pigs."

"Go," Jesus told them; so they left and went off into the pigs. The whole herd rushed down the side of the cliff into the lake and was drowned.

The men who had been taking care of the pigs ran away and went into the town, where they told the whole story and what had happened to the men with the demons. So everyone from the town went out to meet Jesus; and when they saw him, they begged him to leave their territory. (Matthew 8:28-34, GNB)

St. Matthew's account of the men with the demons and the herd of pigs differs from St. Mark's and St. Luke's in a number of ways. In St. Matthew's account, for instance, there are two men–not one–and they terrorize the whole area: "They were so fierce that no one dared travel the area." Since each of the Synoptic Gospel writers discusses the story, it warrants further attention in this discussion of healing. What follows is my personal reflection on the three versions, not a systematic exegesis.

Perhaps in the New Testament era it was not uncommon for men to hide out in burial grounds, away from society. We have been conditioned to remember the lepers as being out and away from communities for health reasons. No doubt, the New Testament era was much like our own, when too many men, women, and children are being thrown onto the streets and forced to survive. The streets of any U.S. city are peopled with men and women who act just like the men in St. Matthew's story. These men Jesus encountered were fierce and angry. They threatened all who came near. Their condition? Who can really say? Perhaps they carried a severe mental illness, and their families disowned them out of pain and burden. Perhaps they carried the awful scars of society's brutality. In the cosmology of the New Testament, they "had demons in them."

In the New Testament, illness is never seen individually. Illness is always connected to the greater scheme of things; in the story above, the illness was related to demons. The demons were powerful and indeed controlled the two men. The men are, in fact, almost irrelevant to the story. The conversation is between the demons and Jesus. The demons are cast out. (We don't even hear about the men afterwards in St. Matthew's Gospel.) Jesus is then confronted by the nearby community. They do not like what he has done. They want him out of there. They do not want the order of things disturbed.

It is not difficult to think of the two men as men who may have suffered from PTSD. They certainly carried many of the diagnostic conditions. Not only were they angry, they acted on their anger by terrorizing all who came into their territory. Not only had they withdrawn from society, they lived in the burial caves, a place of condemnation and defilement for the living. In essence, they became the living dead. They fully expected to be punished for who they were. Townspeople were not grateful for their recovery; they seemed to want things to remain as they were. Could it be that the people did not want to remember what had caused the men to behave like that in the first place?

Those of us who are Vietnam veterans have little trouble imagining the two Gadarene men as Vietnam veterans suffering from PTSD. That these Biblical men should be trauma victims would certainly not be unlikely in that trauma-ridden time and place: Gadara was under occupation by foreign troops; terroristic plots were ongoing; and subwarfare was common. Perhaps the men had been in combat. Or a Roman prison may have shaped them for this life in the burial grounds. Our minds can create all sorts of scenarios, each of which makes these men more real to us.

How are we to understand the healing that took place? In St. Matthew's Gospel, we are not even sure a healing really did take place. We assume there was a healing based on the context of the story itself and on the reaction of the people. Such healing has many implications. Whatever caused you to be here is now finished! What brought you here is now resolved! Whatever created the rage and anger is no longer in charge! You are free to leave this place and live in families and community once again! That which was in the process of destroying you is now itself destroyed! Within this context, it is therefore fitting that in St. Luke's story, the man wants to follow Jesus, but Jesus says to him: "Go back home and tell what God has done for you." The man has been restored to life and community.

THE HELPER AND TRAUMA RELATIONSHIPS

The keynote in any healing process begins, continues, and ends with the relationships among people. As we review the case presentations in this book, we notice that each victim has experienced some type of broken relationship. Those who suffered a broken relationship early in life tend to withdraw deep into their own self. It seems to them that nothing can be trusted.

It is in the formation of relationships that the helper must become expert, recognizing first of all that no one of us can possibly relate in therapeutic ways with all people. This is where we learn a good sense of humility-which must be learned and relearned. This is where we will be put to the test over and over again. Because the hurt of humiliation or physical pain is to be avoided at almost any cost, persons trying to come to a new relationship will indeed present many obstacles to forming a healing relationship (where trust and intimacy are at the core).

The people I have talked about in this book are real, though I have changed their stories enough to protect their integrity and identity. Each came for healing and each had that driving need to avoid changing the status quo in their lives. Each wanted to avoid changing those coping strategies that enabled them to live, albeit restrictedly.

RULES FOR HEALING

The role of the helper of the horrific-traumata victim is to willingly engage in an intimate relationship with the person, while doing no harm. To avoid this inherent danger of harming the person coming for help, there must be the willingness to faithfully adhere to the following two cardinal rules:

1. Know your limitations and the amount and kind of help you are prepared to share with this person out of your own self, training, and background.
2. Share with another professional any and all feelings that you have regarding your helping relationship with a trauma victim. Be honest about your feelings to a fault.

Applying these two cardinal rules will help to reduce, by a significant level, the amount of harm that may be done in a helping relationship. However, the rules do not eliminate harm totally. We need to be closely in touch with our own unconscious processes-through our own psychotherapy or spiritual journey skills, for example-so that we can look long and honestly into our own interior life.

Anyone who works with the severely traumatized should also be able to consult with a number of professionals working in the field. It is also a good idea to find out about treatment facilities that acknowledge and practice good treatment of trauma victims.

THE HEALING PROCESS

As helpers enter into the healing process of others, they must be aware that healing must continue to take place within the life of the helper. Many of us have failed to understand this. When the healing process is maintained within ourselves, then the process of the therapeutic relationship with the other person will also be vital and healing.

Once we enter into an active process where healing takes place, we must also ask some very important questions about the nature of healing. In the New Testament, we see Jesus not only casting out demons and restoring persons to family and community but also restoring physical health: the blind are made to see and the deaf are made to hear. What healing can we offer to those who suffer from severe emotional trauma? We cannot take away the trauma. We cannot take away the scars left by the trauma. Can we restore them to family and community? Can we "bring them back to life?" Can we help them to learn to *live* in spite of wounds that will never heal? Is that enough?

My brother Donald told me recently of seeing a marvelous statue of Lazarus in a parish near Oxford, England. Lazarus has risen from his grave, with his burial cloths draping from his body, and he is looking over his shoulder at the high altar of the church as he walks toward the exit. From that image, I immediately recognized the tension between living in this world and joining the Heavenly Banquet: Is one healed who chooses to come back to finish life in this world?

In a discussion of the question of what is healing, microbiologist René Dubos describes two types of healing.[3] The first involves "returning to the state of health in which the patient was before the disease, that is, correcting the damage that had been done." Dubos does not believe that this type of healing happens very often. The second type of healing is "a very different mechanism, a kind of permanent change in the patient or organism, that makes that patient or organism better capable of coping with whatever new situation has happened." Dubos referred to this second type as "creative adaptation."

Dubos continues by stating that "whatever happens to us, whatever we experience, we respond to it by changing. . . . There is not one experience that you have that does not become incorporated into your nature. You are never the same after having done something or having experienced something. . . . If an infection takes place, the body can develop immunological mechanisms so that there is no trace left of the infection. But there is a trace left in your whole immunological mechanism, such that your immunological mechanism has been marked by that first experience, you will never from now on respond as if you had never had that first experience."

In summary, Dubos writes, "Returning to healing, I want to emphasize that the response of the body, instead of attempting to restore the mind or the body to the condition in which it was before the insult, most commonly, practically always, brings about a lasting change. That change can be deleterious (such as scar tissue in the liver which leads to fibrosis), but the change can be also adaptive, namely, it can be a change in the whole organism that makes that organism different from the way it was before, but much better able in the future to meet new conditions."

Dubos ends his discussion this way: "[T]o heal does not necessarily imply to cure. To heal may simply mean helping the patient to make curative adaptations to any kind of organic deficiencies. This caring as against curing aspect of medicine aims at rehabilitating patients by helping them to achieve a way of life that the patient finds tolerable and productive even in the presence of continuing disease."

Dr. Robert Clayton, a psychiatrist with whom I have worked for years, has often remarked to me: "Just because someone has a disease, that person doesn't have to be sick." This is so very true in the lives of alcoholics and diabetics. It is an important concept for us to remember as we work with victims of severe emotional trauma. We need to keep fully aware of the history of the illness we are dealing with and to have a definition of what will constitute healing under the given circumstances.

Healing within the context of the New Testament is always a restoration to both life and community. A man came to Jesus and said to him, "If you want to, you can make me clean." Jesus reached out and touched him. "I do want to." A woman approached Jesus, saying, "If only I touch his cloak, I will get well." Jesus said: "Courage, my daughter! Your faith has made you well" (Matthew 9:9, GNB).

NOTES

1. Southard, Samuel. "The Emotional Health of the Pastoral Counselor," Wayne Oates, Ed., *An Introduction to Pastoral Counseling* (Nashville: Broadman Press, 1959), p. 43.

2. The series of quotations above are quoted in: *Parabols: Myth and the Quest for Meaning,* Volume xv, Number 1, February 1990).

3. Dubos, Rene. "Self Healing: A Personal History," Robert Ornstein and Charles Swencionis, Eds., *The Healing Brain: A Scientific Reader* (New York: The Guilford Press, 1990), pp. 135ff.

Chapter 8

Pastoral Response–
A View from Scripture

This chapter is a reflection on Holy Scripture and it can perhaps be best used as a springboard for meditation. I originally prepared this discussion for a talk I gave as part of a forum at St. Luke's United Methodist Church in Columbus, Georgia. The forum was on AIDS, and this discussion was an attempt to focus on AIDS from a Biblical perspective. On reflection, I now offer it as the last section of this book on horrific traumata, since Scripture speaks the same language to both catastrophes.

PTSD is first and foremost a spiritual disorder, and healing must necessarily come from within a spiritual context. From the point of view of the pastoral counselor, both the disorder and the healing can be conceptualized Biblically. A Biblical perspective gives particular insight into the trauma, the response to it, its lifelong effect, and the healing from the trauma.

I see PTSD as a spiritual disorder in the sense that PTSD involves the loss of hope, trust, and relationships. This is, of course, the Biblical story: Hope given, hope lost, and hope regained. Paradise given and lost, the twig which blooms out of the fallen dead tree, death and resurrection are at the very essence of the Biblical story in which the reality of lost hope and the promise of hope regained are affirmed over and over again. PTSD care and healing are best undertaken in light of this continuing affirmation.

The Biblical story of everyman (Adam) and everywoman (Eve) begins with Creation. Out of the dirt, out of the rib, creation is fashioned. It is God's stuff and God breathes life into this new creation. The Fall, like Creation, is every person's experience. It is the context from which we all move and function. From a human perspective, the killing of Abel by Cain, and the agony of their parents, is a trauma in which we might begin to see the formation of PTSD symptoms in the heart of the human family. Cain, who was sent to a land called Wandering, said: "I will be a homeless wanderer on the earth" (Genesis 4:13ff, GNB).

The Old Testament–with its stories of exiles, captivities, and exodus–conveys over and over again the loss of hope, trust, and relationships: "Look what you have done by bringing us out of Egypt! Didn't we tell you before we left that this would happen? We told you to leave us alone and let us go on being slaves of the Egyptians. It would be better to be slaves there than to die here in the desert" (Exodus 14:11-12, GNB). The profound loss of hope, the worship of idols (that desperate attempt to fill a void), and the rejection of salvation all afflict humanity when hope, trust, and relationships with God and others are lost.

As we consider the story of Job, we are struck by his wistfulness when he says the words thought or spoken by every PTSD victim: "If only my life could once again be as it was when God watched over me" (Job 29:2, GNB) and "I always expected to live a long life and to die at home in comfort" (Job 29:18, GNB).

Horrific events in the Bible are great in number. A significant episode in the trauma-filled life of King David brings out the reflections of a grief-stricken father: "And the king was much moved, and went up to the chamber over the gate, and wept; and as he went, thus he said, O my son Absalom! Would God I had died for thee, O Absalom, my son, my son" (II Samuel 18:33, GNB). Absalom had led an unsuccessful rebellion against his father, who soon after found him dead, hanging by his hair in the bushes. The horror of David's discovery echoes through all of human history, especially when men have found their sons dead from battle and/or rebellion. Anger and hurt are very often frozen in time and usually unresolved.

"From the depths of my despair I call to you Lord. Hear my cry, O Lord; listen to my call for help" (Psalm 130:1, GNB). It is from this vantage point that the Biblical story continually reminds us that *we must* approach God. "Save me, O God! The water is up to my neck; I am sinking in deep mud, and there is no solid ground; I am out in deep water, and the waves are about to drown me. I am worn out from calling for help, and my throat is aching. I have strained my eyes, looking for your help" (Psalm 69:1-2, GNB).

"And the Word became flesh and dwelt among us!"(John 1:14, GNB). The Incarnational truth of the New Testament restores hope-the hope that is realized when God Himself crawls down into the pit of despair with us to lift us out and carry us to safety.

"Teacher, whose sin caused him to be born blind? Was it his own or his parents' sin?"(John 9:2, GNB). Jesus spit into the dirt and made mud. He then placed the mud on the eyes of the blind man and sent him to the pool to wash. Having done this, the blind man was healed. It has come full cycle now. We are back to the dirt and to the mixture of human and divine. The new creation in Christ is made explicit in the dirt and the spit. Out of this, we are made new creatures in Christ.

"In view of all this, what can we say? If God is for us, who can be against us? Certainly not God, who did not even keep back his own Son but offered him for us all! He gave us his Son–will he not also freely give us all things?" (Romans 8:31-32, GNB).

Surely in all this, God-in-Christ cannot be separated from the sodomized child, the unconscious child beaten by her mother, or the orphan forced to eat her vomited breakfast by the matron who wants to teach her a lesson. To the soldier who has shot his own man to save him from his last hours of agony, Christ is present. "Nothing can separate us from the love of Christ" (Romans 8:35, GNB).

"My dear friends, do not be surprised at the painful test you are suffering, as though something unusual were happening to you. Rather be glad that you are sharing Christ's sufferings, so that you may be full of joy when his glory is revealed" (I Peter 4:12, GNB). This mutual sharing of suffering is the keynote of the Christian message to those who are in the midst of human suffering. The condemnation of those who suffer is revoked and the gentle mutual suffering of Christ and humankind is shared. When Peter and the Apostles were in the midst of their pain, grief, and despair, they went fishing. It was the Jesus, the crucified one, who met them on the beach with a cooked breakfast: "Jesus went over, took the bread, and gave it to them; he did the same with the fish." (John 21:13, GNB).

The ministry, to those who stand in extraordinary pain, is from a Lord who has shared our sufferings and who extends to us all a hope that was forged in the white heat of suffering and in the midst of death and hell itself. It is only a God who has shared our suffering and known our lot who can extend hope: "Now God's home is with mankind! He will live with them, and they shall be his people. God himself will be with them, and he will be their God. He will wipe away all tears from their eyes. There will be no more death, no more grief or crying or pain. The old things have disappeared" (Revelations 21:3-4, GNB). Thanks be to God!

Index

AIDS, 2,113
Alcohol treatment, 16-17
Alcohol abuse, 16
   blackouts, 82
   management of PTSD symptoms,
     17,22,26,42,62,69-70
Alienation, 54-55
American Psychiatric Association, 13
Amnesia,
   national, 18,62
   psychogenic, 36,42
Amnesty, 60
Armstrong, Gloria, 4,85
Arlington National Cemetery, 51
Awe, *x*,43,72

Bhopal, 15
Book of Common Prayer, 22,79,99
Bouncing Betty, 9

Chaim, Shatan, 12-13
Chernobyl, 15
Code of Conduct, 18

Diagnostic and Statistical Manual
     of Mental Disorders (DSM),
     13,35-37,47
Dissociation, 85
Dachau, 51
Descartes, René, 66
Dissonance, perceptual, 13,20
Dreams, 25,29,30-31,33,36,41,42,
     53-54,90-93
Dubos, René, 109-110

Eucharist, 50
Evil, *xvi*, 8,19,45,89,90

Figley, Charles, *xi*, 24,96-97
Flashbacks, *ix*,23,33,36,38-39,
     51,55,69
Freud, Sigmund, 63
Fromm, Erich, 15

Grace, 1,3,4,87-89,91,107
Group therapy, 7,10,35,39,42,61-63,
     85-87

Healing memory, 70
Holocaust, 14,19,24,93
Hurricane Andrew, *xii*,89
Huston, John, 17
Hypervigilance, 37,43
Hypnotherapy, 41

Incest, 1,2,7-8,11,13,15,40-42,53,
     85,89
International Society for Traumatic
     Stress Studies, 13,14
Intimacy, *xii*,41,43,76,101-102,
     104,108
   loss of, *x,* 66,68-69

Journal of Traumatic Stress,
     14,96-97

Kent State University, *ix*,60

Lifton, Robert Jay, 12,23
Little Red Riding Hood, 19

Mark's Dream, 90-93
M.A.S.H., 11
Mason, Steve, 49